*Collegeville Ministry Series*

# THE MINISTRY OF MUSIC
## Singing the Paschal Mystery

Kathleen Harmon, S.N.D. de N.

**LITURGICAL PRESS**
Collegeville, Minnesota

www.litpress.org

Design by Joachim Rhoades, O.S.B. Cover image by Joe Mitchel.

Material in this book has previously appeared in the "Music Notes" column of *Liturgical Ministry*. The first section of part III is based on material which originally appeared in *Lifting Up Jesus Christ: Yesterday, Today and Forever,* copyright © 2001 Evangelical Lutheran Church in America, and is used by permission of Augsburg Fortress.

Excerpts from *Liturgical Music Today* © 1982 United States Conference of Catholic Bishops, Inc., Washington, D.C.; excerpts from *Music in Catholic Worship* © 1983 United States Conference of Catholic Bishops, Inc. Used with permission. All rights reserved.

Excerpts from the *Lectionary for Mass for Use in the Dioceses of the United States of America,* second typical edition © 1998, 1997, 1970 Confraternity of Christian Doctrine, Inc., Washington, D.C. Used with permission. All rights reserved. No portion of this text may be reproduced by any means without permission in writing from the copyright owner.

1       2       3       4       5       6       7       8

**Library of Congress Cataloging-in-Publication Data**

Harmon, Kathleen A., 1944–
      The ministry of music : singing the paschal mystery /
   Kathleen Harmon.
          p. cm. — (Collegeville ministry series)
      Includes bibliographical references (p.    ).
         ISBN 0-8146-2878-8 (pbk. : alk. paper)
            1. Church music—Catholic Church.  2. Ministers of music.
      3. Catholic Church—Liturgy.  I. Title.  II. Series.

   ML3002.H36   2004
   264'.0202—dc22                                           2003018511

# Contents

# Abbreviations

| | |
|---|---|
| CSL | Constitution on the Sacred Liturgy |
| GIRM | General Instruction of the Roman Missal 2002 |
| *LMT* | *Liturgical Music Today* |
| *MCW* | *Music in Catholic Worship* |

# Introduction

On the Twenty-second Sunday of Ordinary Time, Year A, the music director stood up before the beginning of Mass and explained that the Gospel reading of the day (Matt 16:21-27) would be introducing a dramatic shift in our journey with Christ through Ordinary Time. Jesus would begin walking deliberately toward Jerusalem and certain death. Peter would attempt to block his path and Jesus would challenge him in no uncertain terms: if you wish to be my disciple you must follow where I go; only if you do so can you be glorified with me. "Our task throughout all of Ordinary Time," the music director went on to say, "has been to follow Jesus by choosing his way of living as the norm which guides our lives. And so today when Jesus makes this turn toward Jerusalem we choose to turn with him. With him, we say yes to the death to self which salvation requires. We stay the path. And we indicate our choice musically by making a change in the service music we have been singing. Beginning today and for the rest of the Sundays of Ordinary Time we will be singing (here she named the Mass setting we would be using). Our reason for making this shift is not for the sake of musical variety. We make this shift because it is one way of expressing our choice to walk the journey to Jerusalem with Jesus. He has made a turn on the road and we make a turn with him."

After Mass a senior member of the parish told the pastor what he had experienced as he sang the acclamations that morning: "We've always changed things like the *Holy, Holy* at different points in the year, but I've never thought there was any reason for it other than variety. I never realized these changes were connected to the Gospel reading and to our discipleship. I tell you, Father, I sang the *Holy, Holy* this morning with a whole different sense of what I was doing, and I think everyone else did, too."

This vignette reveals the new level of openness many of us have come to concerning the role of music in the liturgy. With forty years of the implementation of the reforms of Vatican Council II behind us the singing assembly is now the norm in most parishes. And as we have grown in our acceptance of the important place of liturgical singing, we have also grown in our need and desire to understand more clearly the theological reasons for it. The "what's" and the "how-to's" have fallen into place and now we hunger for more of the "why."

*The Ministry of Music: Singing the Paschal Mystery* approaches the "why" of liturgical music by drawing on the notion expressed in the Constitution on the Sacred Liturgy that liturgy is ritual enactment of the paschal mystery.[1] It explores liturgical music in terms of how it enables us, the Body of Christ, to enter more fully into this enactment. The "what's" and "how-to's" of music ministry are then developed from this perspective. How do the eucharistic acclamations, the processional hymns and songs, the responsorial Psalm, and the litanies enable us to participate in and surrender to the paschal mystery? What musical and pastoral choices best enable music to fulfill this role? And how does the music form us in a paschal mystery spirituality which shapes daily Christian living and makes the relationship between liturgy and life more evident?

Chapter 1 defines liturgy as ritual enactment of the paschal mystery and lays the theoretical foundation for how liturgical singing contributes to this enactment. Chapters 2 through 6 make this theology practical by addressing its implications for the ministry of liturgical music. Individual chapters examine the acclamations, the processional hymns and songs, the responsorial Psalm, and the litanies used in the eucharistic rite. Chapters 7 through 9 offer pastoral suggestions for selecting music with the liturgical year in mind, developing seasonal sets of service music, and choosing a parish music resource. Finally, Chapter 10 presents a paschal mystery spirituality for liturgical musicians.

## Note

[1] "[T]he Church has never failed to come together to celebrate the paschal mystery . . . celebrating the Eucharist in which 'the victory and triumph of [Christ's] death are again made present,'" (CSL §6 in *Vatican Council II: The Conciliar and Post Conciliar Documents,* ed. Austin Flannery, O.P., new rev. ed. [Northport, N.Y.: Costello, 1992], vol.1). Altogether CSL uses the term "paschal mystery" eight times. The *Catechism of the Catholic Church* reiterates the point: "Christian liturgy not only recalls the events that saved us but actualizes them, makes them present. The Paschal mystery of Christ is celebrated . . . . and in each celebration there is an outpouring of the Holy Spirit that makes the unique mystery present" (New York: Catholic Book Publishing Company, 1994) §1104.

# 1

# Liturgy and the Paschal Mystery

## What Liturgy Is

Often a helpful way to define something is to begin by identifying what it is *not*. First of all, liturgy is not private prayer, although it requires moments of individualized prayer and is always deeply personal. Liturgy is not evangelization, although persons are certainly drawn to faith in Christ because of the quality of our liturgical celebrations. Liturgy is not catechesis, although we certainly grow in understanding truths of our faith because of liturgical celebration. Liturgy is not the celebration of a "feel-good" sense of community that comes from knowing everyone else's name and story, although in every parish subgroups must know this about one another. Liturgy is not (and this will sound heretical to some) our work, although certainly one of the primary recoveries of Vatican II was ownership of the liturgy by all members of the community of the faithful.

First and foremost, liturgy is the work of God. Only secondarily is it our work and even this work is not perhaps what we might assume at first glance. Liturgy is the work of God drawing us to union with the divine Self through the person of Christ in the power of the Spirit. Liturgy is the action of God transforming us more perfectly into being the Body of Christ. Our part of the liturgical action is simply to give ourselves over to being transformed. Such surrender is the highest form of worship, for it comes from a heart that offers not empty sacrifice but willing obedience. Yes, liturgy *is* our work, but this work is that of surrendering, of giving over control rather than grasping it. No easy task, this. But we are led on the way by the One who has gone before us, Christ who gave his body and blood in loving obedience to the will of a Father who desired the world's redemption. The liturgy is our work because it is *first* the work of Christ who gave himself to the point of death and who now leads us to the same point. Moreover, he leads us to this point and beyond. For just as we die with Christ so too will we be raised with Christ to glory (Rom 6:3-8). And here again we discover that the liturgy is first and foremost God's work, for the One who raises from death is God. In every liturgical celebration we surrender with Christ to death and are raised by God to new life.

Pure and simple, then, liturgy is ritual immersion in the paschal mystery. The liturgical act being done is nothing less than God acting to transform us and our surrendering to that transformation by choosing to pass through the doorway of death to new life. Christ leads the way through his own act of self-surrender to the mystery of dying and rising. We follow by choosing—fully, actively, consciously—to surrender ourselves to this paschal mystery as it unfolds within the liturgical rite, and moreover, in the demands of our daily lives.

Most of us understand that the term paschal mystery refers to Christ's life, death, and resurrection. What we are only beginning to grasp, however, is the astounding concept expressed in Rom 6:3-11 that this mystery is *our* mystery, that it is we who live, die, and rise today as the Body of Christ in the world. The paschal mystery is not just a past historical event; it is also a present event occurring in the life of every one of us individually and in the life of the Church as a whole. The paschal mystery plays itself out constantly in our daily lives as we choose fidelity to Christian discipleship by dying to self so that we, and others, may have fuller life. And it plays itself out in liturgy where we celebrate it in ritualized form. Every time we gather for liturgy we are the Church visibly united in communal surrender to this dying and rising mystery which defines our lives. Within and through the rite, we surrender as one body to this redemptive mystery, and as one body we undergo transformation to new life.

This understanding of liturgy, although as old as the Church,[1] is nonetheless revolutionary. As the *Milwaukee Symposia for Church Composers* points out, there is only one theme for every liturgical celebration and that is our full, conscious, and active participation in the paschal mystery of our dying and rising in Christ.[2]

## The Role of Music in the Liturgy

Once we grasp that the core of the liturgy is ritual enactment of the paschal mystery, our understanding of the role of music in the liturgy moves to a new level. Since music holds a constitutive place in the liturgy it must contribute in some fundamental way to this enactment. The single most important role of music in the liturgy, then, is to help us surrender to the paschal mystery as it unfolds within the rite. This concept is revolutionary but also clarifying. The role of music is not to entertain, not to keep us "interested" when the rite seems dry. The music is not an end in itself but a means to our renewal of identity as Body of Christ. How specifically does music contribute to the liturgical enactment of the paschal mystery? In what way does singing engage us in the mystery of dying and rising in Christ which the liturgy is ritualizing? Part of the answer lies in the nature of music itself. The other part lies in our free choice as members of the assembly.

**The nature of music.** First of all music is by nature a constantly renewing cycle of death and resurrection. The instant a tone is sounded it must begin to die so that the next tone may be born. This means that every musical line is a flow of organically related "dyings" and "risings." Moreover, this flow goes someplace. The dyings and risings move toward some musical conclusion, some point of final resolution. In other words, there is a meaning to this on-going cycle of dying and rising. It is not random, but purposeful.

As we sing we release our breath into this purposeful cycle of dying and rising. We become bodily engaged in its rhythm. We latch onto one note only to let it go as our breath moves us on to the next note. The engagement in dying and rising may be unconscious, but the physicality of our breathing is not. We experience its rhythm, its continuous circle of inward flow and outward release. As we sing together this rhythm becomes communal. We begin to breathe as one body. On a level far beneath the surface of the music we become bound to one another in a communal rhythm of dying and rising. We enter through song into the mutuality of our identity as Body of Christ living and breathing the paschal mystery.

Secondly, music is also by nature an encounter between force and resistance.[3] All sound is the product of a force meeting a resistance—the push of wind against tree leaves, for example, or the striking of hammer against piano strings, or the rush of water against stones in a creek bed. With singing this force-resistance encounter begins where our breath pushes against the vocal folds in our larynx. This is a natural dynamic, one in which we unconsciously engage every time we sing. And it is personal: this is our own body acting out of natural force-resistance mechanisms. Whenever we sing with others, however, the force-resistance dynamic occurring within us also operates *among* us. As our individualized voices struggle to become one voice, the force of our own personalities meets the resistance of all the other personalities in the room, and vice versa. All of our resistances to one another—our competitiveness, envy, jealousy, resentment, desire to dominate, etc.—collide with the force of the music itself calling us beyond self-centeredness to common purpose and common identity.

When our singing together is within the context of the liturgy this encounter of force and resistance becomes an embodiment of our ritual enactment of the paschal mystery. The force is simply the movement of grace urging us to surrender our resistance to becoming one body in Christ. There is a dying to self called for here, and each time we choose to undergo it, we rise to a new state of consciousness as Body of Christ—where all barriers between self and others have been melted. We become Body of Christ united in common force against all the resistances in the human heart which impede the movement of the Spirit toward salvation of the world.

This communal surrender to our identity as Body of Christ does not happen, however, without some resistance on our part, and this is part of the mystery of redemption. Just as there can be no singing without physical resistance in the larynx, so there can be no authentic surrender to the paschal mystery without some resistance on our part. The marvel is that the paschal mystery does not obliterate our resistance to dying to self but uses it to enable the very surrender which is required. Truly life rises from death. And the very activity of our singing together liturgically embodies this mystery and enables this transformation.

**Our free choice.** A second part of the answer to the question about how music enables our ritual enactment of the paschal mystery lies within our own hearts, for to join the liturgical assembly in song is to make a choice. The very choice to sing is a revelation of our personal will and intention to engage with the Body of Christ in the ritual enactment of our dying and rising. None of us ever comes to liturgy without resistance; this is the natural human condition. As pointed out above, this resistance is in fact the very stuff which makes our surrender possible. The call of the liturgy is to do the surrendering and by its very nature song facilitates this choice even while we are resisting it. We may not always be conscious of this movement of surrender to the paschal mystery, but we are often conscious of the sense of release, of "giving over" to something beyond ourselves, which singing generates.

The more aware we become of liturgical singing as participation in the dying and rising mystery which the liturgy enacts, the more readily we can allow our singing to facilitate our surrender to this mystery. We will sing, then, not just because we enjoy this particular hymn or this particular setting of the Mass, but because we want to enter with the assembled Church into this dying and rising mystery which marks our identity. Then our communal singing will become a revelation not only of the beauty of the music itself, or of the musical capability of this particular community, but of something far deeper: the transformation of this community into the dying and rising Body of Christ.

Understanding liturgy as ritual enactment of the paschal mystery has implications for the ministry of liturgical music.

First, it becomes clear that the most important ministers of music are the members of the assembly for they are the Body of Christ engaging in the enactment. What most facilitates their full-voiced and full-hearted singing? How do we help them grow in understanding their singing as a ministry? How do we help them see their singing as a paschal mystery activity?

Second, while we need to select liturgical music which is accessible to the people in our given culture and situation, this must be music which can sustain the ritualizing of the paschal mystery. No matter how accessible, music which is simplistic or sentimental is not challenging enough. In a very subtle way, what we are doing when we sing such music is avoiding the Cross. We need to ask not how a given piece of music makes the assembly feel, but how it makes them think and how it invites them to act. Do both text and music challenge them to surrender to the paschal mystery?

Third, we need to teach our choirs to sing more than just the notes on the page. We need to help them grasp that their liturgical singing is an unfolding of the paschal mystery and that their ministry is to model for the assembly what it means to surrender through song to becoming the Body of Christ. We need to help them identify their resistances to becoming Body of Christ so that they can allow God to use these very resistances to enable their transformation.

The chapters which follow explore these musical implications and pastoral applications in greater detail.

### Notes

[1] CSL §6.

[2] *The Milwaukee Symposia for Church Composers: A Ten-Year Report* (Washington, D.C.: The Pastoral Press and Chicago: Liturgy Training Publications, 1992) §28.

[3] The notion of sound as the product of force meeting resistance, and of voice as expression of force-resistance interactions between self and others is taken from David Burrows, *Sound, Speech and Music* (Amherst: University of Massachusetts Press, 1990).

# Defining Liturgical Music

A great deal of music exists which, although religious, is not appropriate for liturgy because that is not that music's intended purpose. We need to make distinctions among the genres of religious music, to understand their varying purposes, and to use them appropriately. We need also to have a clear understanding of what constitutes liturgical music. This chapter defines what liturgical music is by distinguishing it from forms of sacred music which are not liturgical. The chapter then prioritizes liturgical music according to its functions, its forms, and its ministers. Finally, the chapter suggests pastoral implications which flow from understanding the nature of liturgical music and its hierarchies.

## Examples of Nonliturgical Sacred Music

Some sacred music is intended only for concert use. Its texts are religious or scriptural, even liturgical. Examples of sacred concert music are Handel's *Messiah*, Mozart's *Requiem*, and Haugen's *Gospel of Mark*. Also included in this genre are settings of the Mass for chorus, orchestra, and soloists—such as Haydn's *Masses*—which, although used in actual liturgies at the time of their composition, no longer accord with the renewed liturgy of Vatican II. This is not only because of revisions in the liturgical text, but also, and more importantly, because the dominance of choir and soloists in such settings changes the assembly into an audience.

Another category of religious music that is not liturgical is catechetical: songs written to help children internalize the meaning of a Scripture passage or the content of a catechism lesson. These songs are not suitable for liturgy because the purpose of liturgy is not catechesis. Although we do learn about our faith and grow in understanding it through liturgical celebration, the primary goal of liturgy is not teaching but ritual surrender to the paschal mystery. Using music intended for religious education in the liturgy makes liturgy a didactic event rather than a sacramental one.

A third type of nonliturgical religious music is Christian evangelical music. This music readily engenders religious responses within people—feelings of awe, for example, or yearning for God, or closeness to Christ, or sorrow for sin. But because the texts of these songs tend to focus on individual personal experience rather than on ecclesial identity they are best suited for devotional prayer situations such as faith-sharing groups, renewal experiences, or youth ministry retreats, rather than for liturgy.

## Liturgical vs. Devotional Songs

This last category points out the need to distinguish generally between hymns and songs which are liturgical and those which are devotional in style and content. Because hymnbooks are used for more than liturgy most of them contain devotional as well as liturgical songs. Although spiritually uplifting and prayerful, devotional hymns are not appropriate for liturgy because they cannot support the *kind* of prayer which the liturgy requires, that is, prayer which expresses surrender as Body of Christ to the ritual enactment of the paschal mystery. How do we distinguish liturgical hymn texts from devotional ones?

We need to begin by considering the difference between devotional and liturgical prayers. Both are necessary for full Christian spirituality, but they differ in their focus. Devotional prayer centers on our immediate needs and concerns and adapts as these needs change. Liturgical prayer, on the other hand, focuses on the rhythm of the paschal mystery as it unfolds in the life of the Church throughout the liturgical year. Liturgical prayer, then, does not change with our needs, but draws us beyond them to the broader context of the mystery of Christ dying and rising in us. The structure of our devotional prayer is shaped by us, and rightly so. With liturgical prayer, however, the opposite dynamic occurs: we are shaped by the prayer.

In order for these two types of prayer to fulfill their respective roles in Christian living, each has its own form. Because it focuses on immediate needs and on our individual relationship with God or Jesus, devotional prayer is free-form prayer. Whether we are praying alone or with a group devotional prayer allows us to pour out our personal needs and concerns before God. Liturgical prayer, on the other hand, is highly structured. Its content is decided by the Church and spelled out in her ritual books. Its purpose is to take us beyond our individual, immediate concerns and immerse us in the prayer of the universal Church and in our vocation to be the Body of Christ dying and rising for the salvation of the world.

Once we understand the difference between devotional and liturgical prayer it becomes easier for us to distinguish between those songs which are intended for liturgy and those which are better suited for devotional prayer. Devotional song texts speak of personal salvation in terms of our individual relationship with Jesus. Liturgical hymn texts, on the other hand, use ecclesial terminology: they sing of the Church, of the sacraments, of our identity as Body of Christ. They are paschal mystery-oriented, that is, they speak not so much about being saved by the blood of Jesus as about choosing to participate with Christ in the mystery of death and resurrection. They use sacramental rather than devotional language, speaking of Eucharist and baptism in terms of ecclesial relationships rather than in terms of individual salvation and healing.

Consider, for example, these two texts:

> I need thee every hour, most gracious Lord;
> no tender voice like thine can peace afford.
> I need thee, O I need thee; every hour I need thee;
> O bless me now, my Savior, I come to thee.[1]

> Be still, my soul: the Lord is on your side.
> Bear patiently the cross of grief or pain;
> leave to your God to order and provide;
> in every change God faithful will remain.
> Be still, my soul: your best, your heavenly friend
> through thorny ways leads to a joyful end.[2]

Because these texts emphasize our individual relationship with God or Jesus, their content is devotional. They are theologically accurate—and prayerful—but they take us to a place of private, individualized prayer that is not appropriate for liturgy. Their focus is at odds with the communal focus of liturgical prayer.

By contrast, consider these texts:

> At the Lamb's high feast we sing Praise to our victorious King,
> Who has washed us in the tide Flowing from his pierced side;
> Praise we him, whose love divine Gives his sacred Blood
>     for wine,
> Gives his Body for the feast, Christ the victim, Christ the priest.[3]

> There's a wideness in God's mercy Like the wideness of the sea;
> There's a kindness in his justice Which is more than liberty.
> There is plentiful redemption In the blood that has been shed;
> There is joy for all the members In the sorrows of the Head.[4]

> On our journey to the kingdom, Forward goes our pilgrim band;
> Singing songs of expectation, Marching to the promised land.
> Clear before us through the darkness, Gleams and burns the
>     guiding light;
> Pilgrim clasps the hand of pilgrim, Stepping fearless through
>     the night.[5]

Texts such as these are liturgically appropriate because they pull us beyond our individual feelings and concerns into our ecclesial identity. They draw us into the liturgy as a communal, ecclesial act. (Note, however, that what determines suitability is not the absence of "I" language but the ability of the song to lead us into communal liturgical prayer. Properly understood, first person texts such as "What Wondrous Love Is This" and "I Heard the Voice of Jesus Say" do just this.)

As ritual enactment of the paschal mystery, liturgy is demanding prayer. We are often tempted, albeit unconsciously, to slip into devotional prayer during the course of liturgy because it is easier. Our task as liturgical musicians, however, is to assist the assembly to remain faithful to liturgical prayer, and we do so precisely through the music we choose to use at liturgy. Page through your parish music resource(s) and determine which hymns and songs are devotional and which are liturgical. Earmark those which can support liturgical prayer, and begin gradually to phase out of use *at liturgy* those hymns which are better suited for devotional prayer. Notice I said to remove them from use *at liturgy*; unless they are theologically unsound, they needn't—nor should they—be removed from the parish repertoire. The issue is not with their value, or with our need for them in our spiritual lives, but with where and how we use them.

If people are hungry for devotional hymn texts, the parish needs to assess what opportunities for devotional prayer it provides. Are they sufficient to meet the needs of the people? Are they scheduled throughout the year? Do they correlate with and support the liturgical feasts and seasons? One of our tasks as liturgical musicians is to help guide the parish in developing the devotional prayer experiences people need, and to use these as the appropriate times for singing devotional hymns.

## Liturgical Music

Liturgical music stands in a category all its own. Acclamations, responsorial psalms, chants, and litanies are unique musical forms intended explicitly for liturgical use. Hymns and songs are not unique to liturgy but their specific functions within the rite are; a hymn or song suitable for liturgy has a style and a text which fits its particular function. Liturgical music is primarily vocal and uses either the texts of the liturgy itself, or texts drawn from liturgy or Scripture. In relation to the Mass we can prioritize liturgical music according to three hierarchies: function, form, and ministers of music. In the first we look at what each element is meant to do or to achieve within the rite; we look at its placement, at its relationship to other elements, and at its part in the unfolding flow of the liturgy. In the second we consider the musical form of each element in terms of the importance of that form to the rite (keeping in mind that form cannot be separated from function as the one enables the other to achieve its purpose). In the third we prioritize the elements in terms of who performs the music, in other words, who sings and why.

**Hierarchy of function.** The hierarchy of musical function can be defined in more than one way. The following schema decides priority based on how closely a given element of music is connected to the rite. (It must be noted that some musical elements cannot be clearly categorized within this hierarchy. For example, the Glory to God is the rite but is not sung during Advent or Lent; the Lamb of God accompanies the rite of fraction, but need not be sung, etc.)

*1. Music which **is** the rite.* The acclamations—primarily the *Sanctus (Holy, Holy)*, the Memorial Acclamation, the Great *Amen*, and the *Alleluia*/Gospel verse—are examples of music which actually constitute the rite. The acclamations *are* the liturgy; in singing them the assembly enacts the rite. Acclamations are of the highest importance both because of where they occur in the liturgy and because of who sings them. Three parameters determine what musical elements belong in this category: the element uses the liturgical text, it is sung by the assembly, and it is a constitutive part of the liturgical celebration.

*2. Music which **accompanies** the rite.* Second in priority is music which does not necessarily use the liturgical text but which enhances the liturgical action by giving it fuller embodiment. In singing the Entrance hymn which accompanies the procession of ministers into the celebration, for example, the assembly symbolically processes into the celebration with them. In singing the Communion hymn which accompanies the procession to the messianic banquet, the assembly deepens their oneness in Christ.

*3. Music which **is optional.*** Third in priority are musical elements which are optional, such as the singing of a hymn during the presentation of the gifts, or instrumental only music, or music by the choir alone.

**Hierarchy of form.** The liturgy utilizes numerous forms of music, each having its own importance in the rite. In order of relative importance, these forms are:

1. *Acclamations.* Because they constitute the rite and because they are to be sung by the assembly as a whole, the acclamations are the most important musical form in the liturgy.

2. *Processional songs.* The primary processional songs are those which accompany the Entrance and the Communion processions. Their importance derives from the importance of these processions. The *Alleluia*/Gospel verse is sometimes classified as a processional song also, and this is particularly applicable on those solemnities, such as Easter and Pentecost, when we have a Sequence. Originally, the sequences were extensions of the verse before the Gospel, meant to accompany a prolonged procession with the Book of the Gospels. (This would be an excellent way to use them on these solemnities today, rather than the all too common and deadening custom of having the assembly simply read the Sequence aloud).

3. *Responsorial Psalm.* Third in importance is the responsorial Psalm, a dialogue between cantor and assembly. The importance of this form lies in the dialogical relationship of the psalm to the readings, and of the assembly to the Word of God, a relationship which the interaction between cantor and assembly embodies and deepens.

4. *Litanies.* There are three litanies in the eucharistic rite: the *Kyrie,* the Prayer of the Faithful, and the *Agnus Dei (Lamb of God).* These may be sung but need not be.

5. *Ordinary chants.* The ordinary chants are the *Kyrie,* the *Gloria,* the Lord's Prayer, and the *Agnus Dei.* These texts form the Ordinary of the Mass, which remains constant rather than changing from season to season, or feast to feast. They may be sung but need not be (although reciting the *Gloria* is something of a contradiction).

6. *Supplementary songs.* Supplementary songs are optional hymns sung by assembly or choir, for example at the Preparation of the Gifts, after Communion, or as a recessional.

*7. Instrumentals.* Instrumental music may occur as prelude or postlude, at the Preparation of the Gifts, or as supplemental Communion music before or after the assembly hymn. It is incidental music on the same level of importance as optional supplementary hymns.

*8. Presidential prayers.* Last in the hierarchy are the presidential prayers which may or may not be sung. Frequently decisions in this regard depend on the solemnity of the celebration (and the ability of the presider!).

**Hierarchy of ministers of music.** The most important ministers of music are the members of the assembly for it is they who, as Body of Christ, enact the rite. All other liturgical ministers perform their respective roles because they are part of the assembly. This is no less true concerning the ministry of music. The second most significant minister of music is the cantor who leads the assembly in sung response to the Word of God proclaimed in their midst. Third in importance is the music director; fourth, the organist and other instrumentalists; fifth, the presider; and last, the choir. Each of these ministers functions in relation to the primary musical minister, the assembly; that is, each of them finds their ministerial identity in terms of the larger identity of the liturgical Body of Christ.

## Pastoral Implications of These Hierarchies

These hierarchies tell us where we need to focus our energy in planning music for liturgy. Although the hierarchies are not clear cut, and some musical elements fall into more than one category, priorities are nonetheless evident. We must begin first with the music that is the rite and look last at those elements of music which are merely supplemental.

Our starting point needs to be selecting sets of acclamations for each season of the liturgical year. Each set should be seasonally appropriate in terms of style. Each should be musically and culturally accessible to the assembly. And each should be reserved for the season for which it has been selected so that in singing them the assembly will be assisted to enter more deeply into the paschal mystery as it unfolds through the cycles of the Church year.

Setting up such a cycle of acclamations will take time. One must begin with assessing the parish's present repertoire, deciding what should stay and what needs to be "retired." Where there are holes in the repertoire, new possibilities must be researched and examined. Then a plan must be developed for teaching the parish new settings which have been selected. This teaching needs to unfold over a long enough period of time so that one new setting can settle in before another new one is introduced. It could realistically take five years to select and teach a full cycle of seasonal acclamations. Once these settings are in place, they should then be left in place so that over time the assembly will know them by heart, will associate them with specific seasons, and will sing them spontaneously. (See chaps. 7 and 8 for a more detailed process for selecting seasonal service music.)

A second priority which emerges from these hierarchies is that we should concentrate most of our attention and energy on developing the primary ministers of music, the assembly. Among other things this means leading them to understand the functions of music within the liturgy. One way of doing this is to institute a regular "Liturgical Music" paragraph in the weekly bulletin. You might begin, for example, with a question and answer scenario like this:

> What is an acclamation? Church liturgy documents tell us that the most important sung parts of the Mass are the acclamations. An acclamation is a short, sung statement of faith and of assent. During the Eucharistic Prayer at Mass, for example, we sing, "Christ has died, Christ is risen, Christ will come again!" Just reading these words probably brings to your mind the melody we use when we sing them. The melody is energetic, uplifting, easy to remember and sing. This is because the acclamation itself is short and to the point. When we sing it we are affirming our belief in Christ and recommitting ourselves to participate with him in the mystery of his death and resurrection.

You might follow up with this blurb the second week:

> During Mass we sing four acclamations, four short, sung statements of faith and assent. The first we sing is the Gospel Acclamation, our *Alleluia* response to the presence of Christ in the

Gospel. By singing it we witness to our belief in his presence and renew our commitment to listen to his Word and let it shape our lives.

During subsequent weeks, write about each of the other acclamations. Keep each statement brief. Communicate just one concept at a time, and repeat ideas often.

While this parish-wide communication is going on, do similar education with your choir. For the first full year focus just on the notion of acclamation. Using computer graphics, print up the four Memorial Acclamations and hang them on the wall in the choir room for the year. Hang up the *Alleluia* also, and the *Sanctus*. Spend a few minutes of each rehearsal talking with the choir about what an acclamation is, and why we sing them in the liturgy. Sing through different sets and get their input about which best fits which season.

## Concluding Remark

Identifying what music is liturgical and placing our attention first on its most important form (the acclamations) and its most important ministers (the assembly) will focus our musical decision making. Choosing hymns and songs, deciding when to sing the *Kyrie,* selecting instrumental and choral preludes, for example, will fall more quickly into place because we will have focused on the right music. In doing so we will be doing far more than just selecting music. We will be surrendering ourselves to the power of the liturgy to transform us ever more fully into the Body of Christ living the paschal mystery, and we will be channeling the power of music to serve this purpose.

## Notes

[1] "I Need Thee Every Hour," Annie S. Hawks, 1872.

[2] "Be Still, My Soul," Katharina von Schlegel, 1752.

[3] *"Ad reglas agni dapes"*; Latin, fourth century, trans. Robert Campbell, 1814–1868.

[4] "There's a Wideness in God's Mercy," Frederick W. Faber, 1814–1863.

[5] "On Our Journey to the Kingdom," Bernhardt Severin Ingemann, 1789–1862, trans. Sabin Baring-Gould, 1834–1924, alt.

# Singing the Acclamations

There are a number of places in the celebration of Mass where short phrases of text are spoken back and forth between a liturgical minister and the assembly. Some are greetings, such as *The Lord be with you—And also with you*. Some are commands, such as *Lift up your hearts—We lift them up to the Lord* and *The Mass is ended, go in peace—Thanks be to God*. Some are litanic responses such as *Kyrie eleison . . . Kyrie eleison* and *Lamb of God, you take away the sins of the world: have mercy on us*. Some are psalms sung in responsorial fashion between cantor and assembly. And finally, some are acclamations.

This chapter examines the acclamations, explores their meanings in terms of both liturgical participation and Christian identity, and suggests what spirituality they engender for Christian self-understanding and paschal mystery living. The chapter then proposes ways the musicality of the acclamations can be better honored.

## Where the Acclamations Are

The General Instruction of the Roman Missal 2002 (hereafter GIRM) may contain a surprise for many in terms of what it identifies as acclamations used in the eucharistic rite. We are well versed in defining the acclamations as four: the *Alleluia*/Gospel verse; the *Holy, Holy*; the Memorial Acclamation; and the Great *Amen*. But GIRM in fact presents us with a larger list. The people's *Amen* to the presidential prayers

(Opening Collect, the Prayer over the Gifts, and the Prayer after Communion) is identified as an acclamation (§§54, 89, 146). The response *Thanks be to God* after the first and second readings is named an acclamation (§§128, 130). The responses both *before* and *after* the proclamation of the Gospel are called acclamations (§§60, 134). Finally, the doxology which concludes the Our Father is identified as an acclamation (§153).

## What the Acclamations Do

GIRM offers some terse but rich commentary about what the assembly is doing in pronouncing the acclamations. By saying *Amen* they take ownership of the prayers and give their personal assent to them (§§54, 89). Through the acclamations surrounding the Gospel they acknowledge Christ alive and present in the proclamation (§60). And through the acclamations intrinsic to the Eucharistic Prayer they join in the proclamation of the story of salvation and offer themselves together with Christ to the Father (§§78–79).

GIRM makes no comment about the acclamations which follow the first and second reading nor about the doxology which concludes the Lord's Prayer. But the fact that GIRM designates these texts as acclamations gives them a unique significance in terms of the rite and of the assembly's role in the rite, for the acclamations are actions which the assembly "are to contribute in every form of the Mass" (§35). Indeed both *Music in Catholic Worship*[1] (hereafter *MCW*) and *Liturgical Music Today*[2] (hereafter *LMT*) list the doxology to the Lord's Prayer as one of the primary acclamations "which ought to be sung even at Masses in which little else is sung" (*MCW* §54; see also *LMT* §17). Such directives suggest that perhaps we need to take a deeper look at the nature of the acclamations and their function in the rite.

## What an Acclamation Is

*MCW* describes the acclamations as "shouts of joy which arise from the whole assembly as forceful and meaningful assents to God's Word and Action" (§53). *LMT* defines the acclamations as "short, direct and strong declarative statement[s] of the community's faith" (§11). But examination of the texts and functions of all the responses which GIRM classifies as acclamations suggest a further, and very significant, dimension to these definitions.

One way to begin uncovering this added dimension is to look at some short, direct statements in the liturgy which are *not* acclamations. For example, some short, direct statements in the rite are dialogues. In verbalizations such as *The Lord be with you—And also with you* an interchange occurs in which the people's response is directed to the minister who initiates the dialogue. Acclamations on the other hand, although always a response to some invitation, prayer, or prior acclamation by presider, lector, or deacon, are shouts of the assembly directed toward God.

For another example, the responsorial Psalm refrains are short, direct, and sometimes declarative, but their purpose is meditation rather than acclamation. The responsorial Psalm refrains are either addressed to God as prayers or to the people as invitations to offer prayer or praise. Some responsorial Psalm refrains are meditations on God and God's ways, some are promises of redemption to those who seek God or remain faithful to the covenant, still others are invitations to praise God or to seek God's help. When addressed to God they are generally petitionary cries, and never acclamatory shouts. Even in the one case (and there is only one case in the entire three-year cycle of psalms) where the psalm refrain is acclamatory in content—*Glory and praise forever!* for Trinity Sunday, Year A—it is still not acclamatory in intent.

## Acclamations as Direct Address to God

Even when cloaked in declarative language or appearing to be a dialogue between members of the assembly acclamations are in reality statements of direct address to God. The *Amen* which concludes the Collects and the Eucharistic Prayer, in each case, is the assembly's participation in the direct address of these prayers to God. The acclamations which conclude the first and second readings are shouts of thanksgiving to God for giving the Word. The acclamations which surround the proclamation of the Gospel—*Glory to you, Lord* and *Praise to you, Lord Jesus Christ*—are direct addresses to Christ, Word of God made flesh among us. The texts of the *Holy, Holy* and the Memorial Acclamation (with the exception of Form A, *Christ has died, Christ is risen, Christ will come again* which transforms the Latin's direct address into a declarative statement[3]) are all in second person direct address form.

What marks the acclamations as acclamations, then, is that they are a *unique and highly potent form of direct address to God*. Sometimes God the Father is addressed, other times, the Second Person of the Trinity, Christ is addressed, but always as the giver of redemption and the initiator of this here-and-now liturgical action. The acclamations are unique in that in them the gathered community most clearly speaks with one voice and one identity as the one Body of Christ. They are unique in that they are the assembly's highest mode of priestly participation in the eucharistic celebration. Other sung elements are also modes of assembly participation, but the acclamations are even more so because it is through their mode of direct address that the assembly stands face-to-face with God in the great act of redemption. In the acclamations the assembly speaks directly to God not as slave or servant, but as friend and collaborator in the ongoing action of mutual self-surrender which is the core of redemption—its wellspring and energizing heart.

Throughout the rite these acclamations enable the assembly to *take ownership of their baptismal identity* by standing in direct address before the One who initiates and desires this identity. To understand this point more clearly consider, for example, the acclamatory *Amen* which concludes each of the presidential prayers. It is not an arbitrary tag-a-long but an essential part of the prayer. The Collects begin with a moment of silence during which assembly members individually raise their hearts and intentions to God. The presider then "collects" these silent prayers into a communal one which he speaks on the community's behalf. The *Amen* is their conclusion to this common prayer, their acknowledgment that they are the one Body of

Christ gathered in petition before the all-redeeming God, their ownership of priesthood in Christ and with one another. This *Amen* is no small thing, no merely murmured second thought, no perfunctory period to someone else's prayer. It is ownership of the prayer and of the personal identity out of which the prayer arises.

Furthermore, in each case, the *Amen* parallels the Great *Amen* which concludes the Eucharistic Prayer, the high point and climax of the entire rite (GIRM §§30, 78). They are, in a sense, a "practice run" for the Great Prayer and its concluding acclamation. This prayer, as the Collects themselves, is the prayer of the entire assembled people who through the leadership and voice of the presider "join [themselves] with Christ in confessing the great deeds of God and in the offering of the Sacrifice" (§78).

The assembly participates in the Great Prayer through both silence and acclamation. In other words, the kind of listening called for is not tepid, half-hearted, or semi-attentive but warm-blooded and fully engaged. The assembly shouts *Amen* because they are the ones offering and being offered, they are the ones being transformed into the Body of Christ, they are the ones being given for the life of the world (§95).

In short, the acclamations celebrate the full maturity God desires for the baptized. They are the assembly's ritual acknowledgment of the dignity and power bestowed upon them by divine plan. In their *Amen* to the collects they make the prayer their own. In their acclamations before and after the readings they make the Word their own. In their acclamations during and concluding the Eucharistic Prayer they make the great offering of Christ their own. They lay themselves upon the altar in the supreme fulfillment of their shared priesthood, offering and being offered, giving and being given, consuming and being consumed. It is no wonder GIRM prescribes that the acclamations be an essential assembly contribution to every celebration of the Mass.

## Spirituality Engendered by the Acclamations

If the acclamations are the assembly's act of direct address to God, what effect does pronouncing them have on our self-understanding and our manner of living out our baptismal identity? In a unique and profound way voicing the acclamations is an act of taking ownership of ourselves. The acclamations teach us that beneath all prayer—whether cries for help, or prayers for healing, or confessions of sin, or words of thanksgiving—stands the empowerment of our baptismal right to address God face-to-face. When we sing the acclamations we dare the one gesture forbidden mere mortals—to look directly upon the face of God—and we discover in that act, not death, but dignity.

Once we understand what we are doing ritually in the acclamations, we can never again look upon self or others in a demeaning way, nor can we ever again approach life's challenges with a sense of disempowerment. Instead we see in self and others the dignity bestowed by God, and we act toward both with reverence and appreciation. And we interpret events—both personal and social, both close at hand and worldwide—not as interventions or judgments of a distant God but as invitations to engage our power with God's in the mutual work of redemption. In short, we grow to full stature before God and with maturity take on our share of responsibility for the coming of the kingdom.

We take for granted that we know what the acclamations in the eucharistic rite are. And we take for granted that these elements are to be sung. But a careful reading of GIRM yields a surprise which can lead us to a deeper understanding of the nature and role of the acclamations and why it is that the Roman Rite is one of acclamation rather than, as with other traditions, of hymnody or of choral anthem. What at first sight can appear to be a musically minimalist approach to liturgy—making musical high points out of short phrases scattered throughout the rite—emerges on closer examination to be an intensely participatory engagement not only in the liturgical celebration but in all of Christian living.

We need to move beyond trite and assumed understandings by taking a fresh look at the acclamations and their significance. We need to understand that the acclamations are acts of liturgical self-possession which catalyze baptismal identity and mission. These reflections here are only a beginning. We must now look at the musical nature of the acclamations and how we might sing them more effectively.

## Singing the Acclamations Well

Because they engender a spirituality which deepens our sense of identity as daughters and sons given the birthright to speak directly to God and to act with God as copartners in the coming of salvation, the acclamations are perhaps the element of the rite which most tellingly celebrate our stance before God as collaborators in the process of redemption and sharers in the identity and mission of Christ. Through them we assert our identity as a people baptized to stand tall, to stand up against evil, to stand forth for justice, and to stand face-to-face with God, aware of our dignity and empowerment.

What follows explores ways of implementing the singing of the acclamations in actual practice. The content unfolds sequentially, looking at the acclamations in the order of their appearance in the rite and proposing ways we can honor their musicality and assist our assemblies to grow in awareness of their meaning and importance.

**The *Amen* to the Collects.** GIRM catagorizes the *Amen* which concludes each of the Collects as acclamations (§§54, 89, 146). In every case, we can better appreciate the significance of the *Amen* when we realize that each of them occurs at a summary point in the rite: the conclusion of the Entrance, the conclusion of the Preparation of the Gifts, and the conclusion of the Communion Rite. These *Amen*s attest to a progressive transformation which is taking place within us.

The Opening Prayer is the final element of the Introductory Rites whose purpose has been to enable us to become aware of our communal identity and open ourselves to hearing the Word of God and celebrating the Eucharist together (GIRM §46). The text of the Collect is always related to the Sunday or season of the year and the readings of the day (what GIRM calls the "character of the celebration"; see §54). What, then, are we saying in our *Amen* to this Opening Prayer? We are saying yes to the working of God within us in terms of this liturgical celebration, we are announcing our readiness to enter into this transformative activity with God. In a sense all the other elements of the Introductory Rites lead up to this *Amen* through which we declare: We are here and we are ready for this celebration; so be it!

The Prayer over the Offerings finalizes our preparation for the Eucharistic Prayer (GIRM §77). The prayer summarizes our readiness to enter once again into the retelling of the story of our salvation. Through our *Amen* we proclaim: We, the gifts, are ready for the great prayer of offering and transformation; so be it!

The Prayer after Communion petitions God "for the fruits of the mystery just celebrated" (GIRM §89). By our *Amen* we declare: We have become one with Christ and with one another; may we remain so and may our living bear testimony to this deepest level of our identity; so be it!

Understood in this light we see that these three *Amen*s parallel and reiterate the Great *Amen* which concludes the Eucharistic Prayer, the climax of the entire liturgy. We see that these *Amen*s are not quietly mumbled responses or barely audible afterthoughts but acclamatory affirmations of our readiness to enter fully into the presence of God and into our baptismal identity. How powerful, then, when these *Amen*s are sung with full-throated, conscious awareness. The style of singing need not be embellished; the standard, well-known two-toned formula is apt expression of the straightforwardness of their incremental intent: Yes, we are here; Yes, we are ready; Yes, we know who we are and who we want to be.

Yet how many assemblies merely mumble these *Amen*s as afterthoughts or as parenthetical interjections? What can we do to help them better celebrate these *Amen*s? First and foremost the Collects need to be well led and this responsibility falls on the shoulders of the presider. This means the presider needs to *pray* the text and not merely read it. He needs to allow the assembly the moment of silence which is to occur between his *Let us pray* and the Collect itself. And he needs to pray the text "musically." Optimally, this means to sing it, but even a presider who lacks the skill or confidence to sing can render the

Collect in a musical way by allowing its natural rhythms and cadences to guide how it is spoken. When the assembly becomes caught up in these rhythms and cadences, when they hear the praying of the presider, they are enabled to enter more easily into the prayer. Sung or spoken their *Amen* then becomes the strong and spontaneous acclamation it is meant to be.

**Acclamations in the Liturgy of the Word.** GIRM indicates that the *Alleluia*/Gospel verse is not the only acclamation marking the Liturgy of the Word; rather, the responses to all three readings are acclamations (§§128 and 130; 60 and 134). We are well versed in understanding the *Alleluia*/Gospel verse as the primary assembly shout in the Liturgy of the Word. In practice, however, how often do we integrate our singing of it with its intent? The *Alleluia*/Gospel verse proclaims the Person of Christ, present in the proclamation of the Gospel. The custom of using the Book of the Gospels rather than the Lectionary for this proclamation further highlights our belief. Yet how commonplace it is that our singing of the acclamation accompanies not the elevation of the Book of the Gospels but the personal and private preparations of the presider or deacon who is to proclaim. GIRM itself is at fault for misleading us. By directing the presider to bow to the altar and say his silent prayer of preparation during the singing of the acclamation (§132) GIRM misdirects our attention. What a difference it would make for our understanding if our first shout of *Alleluia* coincided with the elevation of the Book of the Gospels from its place of repose, and if our continued singing accompanied the procession of the Book to the place of proclamation. How clear the connection would then become between what we were singing and why we were singing it.

The Liturgy of the Word is filled with other acclamations as well, such as the *Thanks be to God* which follows the first and second readings. Through them we express our faith in the presence of God as well as our gratitude for the gift of the Word. But the norm of singing these acclamations raises a pastoral problem, for the assembly can only effectively sing the response if the lector first sings the lead-in. But how many lectors are competent to do so?

What we need to do is teach lectors to proclaim "musically" by letting the sound of their proclamation come from deep within their bodies. All sound carries a dual modality, a directional one which comes from an identifiable source, and an enveloping one which surrounds us with resonance. A proclamation is "dead" when the word neither moves out from its source nor surrounds us with its power. "Musical" proclamation, on the other hand, intensifies both of these modalities.

One way to begin is by helping your lectors learn how to "breath the word." Have them sit quietly, feet flat on the floor, torso upright. Direct them to take in a deep breath, a "belly breath" that is below the belt, then slowly to release it. Have them repeat this deep, intentional breathing a few times until they are comfortable with it. Next direct them to hold the text of the Scripture reading in front of their eyes, reminding them to keep their feet flat and their torsos upright. Direct them to take in a phrase of text silently with a deep breath, then to release the phrase aloud on a slow exhalation of that breath. The goal here is not how long a phrase to take in and then release, nor how slowly or quickly to do it, but how to *connect both the receiving and the giving of the word with one's breathing.* Eventually both the rate of deep breathing and the amount of text taken in visually will increase, but in the early stages of learning this skill it is essential to progress slowly in order that the lectors *physically* experience the sense of connection between words and breath, which is the goal. Regularly spending some time practicing this way will lead over time to a more directional and resonant manner of proclamation. The text will move from being words read off a page to Word of God delivered from deep within the self. This is "musical" proclamation and when the assembly hears it they will listen "musically," letting the personal resonance which is touching them set off echoing vibrations deep in their own bodies and hearts.

**Acclamations during the Eucharistic Prayer.** Through the *Holy, Holy* the assembly joins their voices with the heavenly choir in proclaiming the glory and majesty of God who is sovereign over all things. Scholars believe this prayer was a regular part of the Jewish morning synagogue service where the pas-

sage from Isaiah 6:3 was concluded with the text of Ezekiel 3:12:
". . . I heard behind me the noise of a loud rumbling as the
glory of the LORD rose from its place." This verse referred to the
*Shekinah*, the shining presence of God first localized in the taber-
nacle, then in the Temple. After the exile and the destruction of
the Temple, rabbis began to teach that where two or three were
gathered to read the Word of God, the *Shekinah* stood in their
midst. Early Christian communities transformed this Ezekiel
verse into *Blessed is he who comes in the name of the Lord. Hosanna
in the highest!* Thus the coming of the kingdom and the fulfillment of redemption became united with the notion of Christ as
the true *Shekinah*. The Gospel of Matthew makes this connection
when it has Christ say "where two or three are gathered together in my name, there am I in the midst of them" (18:20).[4]

The Memorial Acclamation "proclaim[s] the mystery of
faith."[5] Although its placement can lead us to misconstrue its
intent, what we acclaim in singing is not the consecratory moment but the entire mystery of salvation, the mystery of God
become flesh that we who are flesh might become like God.
Note that with differing emphases all four forms of this acclamation celebrate the mystery of Christ's death, resurrection,
and return in glory. The texts are summary statements of the
story of salvation. The Memorial Acclamation is addressed to
Christ and proclaims he is alive, even though he has died, and
that he will return in glory.

The Great *Amen* is the assembly's resounding "so be it!" to
the story. Proclaimed in all liturgies between the fourth and
eighth centuries, the Great *Amen* was considered the epitome of
the assembly's participation in baptismal priesthood. This belief was so strong in fact that some argued rebaptism was not
necessary for persons seeking entrance into the Church from an
heretical sect—participation in the Eucharistic Prayer and its
Great *Amen* was proof enough of their identity in Christ.[6]

The assembly singing of the eucharistic acclamations is so second nature to post-Vatican II Catholics that commenting on the
necessity of singing them seems superfluous. Yet in how many
parishes are they not sung full-heartedly, spontaneously, confi-
dently? A number of musical practices are at fault here. I once

experienced one of these to its extreme when I spent a week in a parish where the organist used a different musical setting for the acclamations every day. No one sang because no one knew what to expect. One musical principle concerning the singing of these acclamations is to be consistent in the musical setting we use for them. And the best way to do that is to pair specific settings with specific seasons of the liturgical year. Select one, for example, which fits the celebratory mood of Easter and reserve it for use only during that season, then use it throughout the period. Select another which suits the somber mood of Lent and do the same. You will not only be assisting your assembly to sing these acclamations with spontaneity and assurance, but you will also be helping them to enter the season more fully.

A second musical practice at fault here is overemphasis on learning new songs and hymns at the expense of devoting energy to developing a solid core of seasonal acclamations. Another experience of mine is illustrative here. At the conclusion of a presentation I was making on the priority of the acclamations in the eucharistic rite, a participant exclaimed, "Wow, I've sung in the choir more than twenty years and we never pay attention to the acclamations. Never practice them, never discuss their significance. The most our director ever does is yell a last minute reminder about what acclamations we are singing as we rush from the choir room to the church. I'm realizing now that the acclamations are the first thing we should practice every week and the first thing we should make sure of when we warm up just before Mass."

In our preparation of the choir, in our formation of the assembly, and in our teaching of liturgical music to children and youth we need to focus first on the acclamations and secondarily on other music. Just think of the vibrancy this approach would bring to our liturgical celebrations, a vibrancy born from deeper participation in the core of the rite.

**Doxology to Lord's Prayer.** This doxology, taken from the second-century church document the *Didache,* has long been the tradition in most Eastern churches and among Protestants. GIRM categorizes it as an acclamation and MCW reiterates this stance (§§53–54), but in actual practice we make little of this classification. We simply do not treat this doxology as an acclamation. This is probably due to an intuitive sense of the secondary importance of the Our Father in relation to the Eucharistic Prayer. However, when we do sing the Our Father it is certainly incomplete without the singing of the doxology.

Two musical principles apply. First, the setting should not musically overshadow or compete with the eucharistic acclamations. This is a hard one to avoid because the Lord's Prayer, as many contemporary musical settings reveal, readily lends itself to a style of rendition which is reminiscent of Broadway with its sweeping lines and huge intervallic leaps. The beguiling trap of this style is that it impedes our entry into the deeper regions of ritual celebration by detouring us along the pathway of popular culture. In how many parishes, for example, are the acclamations limp and wimpy while the singing of the Our Father is emotionally robust? We need to ask why this is so, and to examine what we are doing or not doing to allow our ritual to be countercultural.

The second musical principle is that the setting we use needs to be accessible to every member of the assembly. This is also a difficult one to implement, for those who gather every Sunday typically come from such diverse backgrounds that common ground is nonexistent. The resolution, I think, is to pick a simple, singable setting and stick with it. It is not as ritually important to adapt the settings of the Our Father and its doxology to the changing liturgical seasons as it is to line up sets of eucharistic acclamations which change with the seasons. What best facilitates the participation of visitors and reluctant singers in a setting of the Lord's Prayer (and in the eucharistic acclamations, as well) is being surrounded by the strong, confident singing of the other members of the assembly.

## Acclamations and the Mission of the Church

The acclamations are a direct result of Vatican II's recovery of the priesthood of all the baptized and the essential nature of the liturgy as the celebration of all the people. They are *actions* in the form of song. I mentioned above that sound impacts us in a dual way. It is both directional, coming from an identifiable source, and enveloping, encircling us on all sides. Music naturally intensifies both these modes. As the ancient adage states, to sing is to pray twice. We are more present when we sing, more attentive, more participative, and more effective. This is because the song enfolds each member of the assembly with the voices of all the other members of the assembly. We sing the acclamations, then, not only to address God but also in order to direct personal support to one another in living out our identity and mission as Body of Christ. The singing of the acclamations is neither neutral nor inconsequential for it embodies in an intense way the triple directedness of the liturgy toward God, toward our fellow members in Christ, and toward the world. Our singing of the acclamations amplifies their energy and intent: their sound moves out from each of us as individual source, encircles all of us in mutual support, and sends us as community on mission. The more we do, then, to help our assemblies understand the importance of the acclamations and the more we do to enable them to sing the acclamations well, the more we will both deepen their participation in liturgy and their living out of the mission of the Church.

## Notes

[1] *Music in Catholic Worship*, 2nd ed. (Washington, D.C.: United States Catholic Conference, 1983).

[2] *Liturgical Music Today* (Washington, D.C.: United States Catholic Conference, 1983).

[3] See Robert Cabié, *The Eucharist*, vol. 2, *The Church at Prayer*, ed. A. G. Martimort, rev. ed. (Collegeville, Minn.: The Liturgical Press, 1986) 208. The French text reads "We proclaim your death, Lord Jesus; we celebrate your resurrection; we await your coming in glory," and the German reads "We proclaim your death, Lord, and we extol your resurrection, until you come in glory."

[4] See Louis Bouyer, *Liturgical Piety* (Notre Dame, Ind.: University of Notre Dame Press, 1955) 134–35.

[5] See Eucharistic Prayer.

[6] Bouyer, 106.

# Singing Hymns and Songs

Outside of the Liturgy of the Hours the connection of hymns to Roman Catholic liturgy is hazy. Musical elements such as acclamations and litanies belong to the eucharistic rite, but the hymns we sing are actually replacements of what were once the ritual propers of the *Introit,* the Offertory, and the Communion Psalms. For centuries the processional moments in the rite (the Entrance, the Offertory, and the Communion Rite) were accompanied by the singing of psalms specifically assigned to the season or feast day. As the liturgy became the province of the clerics who could read Latin, the people lost their participative role. Not surprisingly the people filled this void by singing devotional hymns during Mass. Officials of the Church responded by outlawing that practice. In 563 the First Council of Braga pronounced: "It is decided that except for the psalms or other parts of the canonical writings of the old and new testament no poetic composition may be sung in church."[1] Even today some liturgists debate the appropriateness of singing hymns during the eucharistic celebration, pointing out that their form often actually interferes with their function, as when the presider's arrival at his chair signals the conclusion of the Entrance procession but the strophic structure of the hymn requires that we keep singing it.

Regardless of this debate, however, hymn singing at the processional moments in the Mass is part of our common practice. Despite the Council of Braga—and with the blessings of the legacy of Vatican II—we Catholics sing hymns at Mass.

Hymns, however, are a very different form of music from the other musical elements we sing. The acclamations, the responsorial Psalm, the *Kyrie*, and *Lamb of God*, for example, are universally legislated. Even options permitted in these texts are limited and controlled. They are not up for grabs. No matter what the culture, country, or language, Roman Catholics throughout the world sing the same acclamations, the same responsorial Psalms, and the same litanies at their eucharistic celebrations. Hymns, on the other hand, are not universally legislated but locally chosen. Their texts are not set but fluid and diverse, constantly changing as human experience changes, theological understandings shift, and multicultural interaction increases.

Moreover, unlike the acclamations, hymns are media for both liturgical and devotional prayer. We sing them alone in the car, in the shower, at private times of personal sorrow or great joy as readily as we sing them with the assembly at liturgy. And although many litanies are prayed as part of devotional prayer the litanies found in the eucharistic rite (the *Kyrie*, the General Intercessions, and the *Lamb of God*) are not in this same category. They can be, but my point is that while we might sing "How Great Thou Art" in the shower, we probably never sing the *Kyrie* while shampooing.

These factors point out how judicious we must be in selecting the hymns we use in the liturgy. This chapter looks briefly at the many forms of processional music available to us today. Then it discusses the role of the processional hymns and songs as catalysts of movement through the rite. Finally, it offers some guidelines and principles to govern the use of hymns and songs.

## Forms of Processional Music

**Hymns.** The word "hymn" is derived from the Greek *hymnos* which meant a song of praise about a god, a hero or heroine, or the marvelous deeds enacted by that god or heroic person. Christians as early as the first century adopted this Greek musical form to sing about the person, deeds, and glory of Christ. Thus Augustine defined a hymn as "a song of praise to Christ."

Christians ever since have written and sung hymns in praise of God and God's wondrous deeds on behalf of human salvation.

But a hymn is not only a song about God. It is also a song about us, about our experience of God and our response. Austin Lovelace offers this definition: "A hymn can be defined as a poetic statement of a personal religious encounter or insight, universal in its truth, and suitable for corporate expression when sung in stanzas to a hymn tune."[2] A hymn begins, then, with us and our experience. The experience is personal, real, close to home. Although it cannot be fully captured in words it can be articulated through poetic means in such a manner that others identify it as authentic Christian experience. Thus while a hymn arises from personal experience, its text is not privatized. The gathered community—in touch with its own experience of God and God's saving actions, and steeped in the inherited experience of the whole Church—can sing the text with authenticity and with assent.

In sum we can say that a hymn is a religious poem meant to be sung congregationally. Linguistically, it is a poetic text using imagery and rhyme to convey its ideas and meaning. Structurally, it unfolds strophically in verses of even length, each line moving according to a selected poetic meter. This structure allows it to be easily tied to a melody of identical meter and length. It is the regularity of length and meter which makes a hymn so easy to sing communally. It is the authenticity of its connection to real faith experience which enables the community to believe what they are singing.

The hymn is a highly structured form constrained by the demands of poetic meter, versification, and rhyme. Meter and rhyme make its text easy to remember. Combined with whatever poetic imagery is used, they also move its train of thought forward for the thought content of most hymns marches deliberately from beginning line through subsequent stanzas to ending line. Generally a central idea or narrative is developed and each stanza has its part to play. A hymn, then, needs to be given full scope to deliver its meaning. One cannot eliminate stanzas without threatening the integrity of the text.

**Nonhymn forms.** In addition to hymns we have a multiplicity of other musical forms available for liturgical use which do not follow hymn structure, e.g., contemporary songs, responsorial pieces, ostinatos, Taizé chants, call and response music, mantras, etc. Many, such as Lucien Deiss' "Grant to Us, O Lord" and Bob Hurd's "Gather Your People, O Lord," are in verse-refrain format. Others such as Marty Haugen's "Bread to Share" and the Dameans' "Table Prayer" are call-response songs requiring a lot of interaction between cantor (or choir) and assembly. Others, like John Bell's "Take, O Take Me as I Am," are simple mantras, short pieces repeated numerous times to induce quiet presence and sustained prayer. The music of Taizé includes verse-refrain songs such as "Eat This Bread," mantras such as "Jesus, Remember Me," and ostinato pieces such as "Laudate Dominum" in which the assembly continuously sings a refrain against or under the singing of verses by cantor or choir. Finally, multiculturalism and globalization have introduced a wide genre of multilingual songs some of which like Cesário Gabaráin's "Una Espiga/Grains of Wheat" are hymnic in their versification, some like Jaime Cortez' "Somos el Cuerpo de Cristo/We Are the Body of Christ" are verse-refrain, some like Donna Peña's "I Say 'Yes,' Lord/ Digo 'Si,' Señor" are call-response, and some like the South African "Mayenziwe/Your Will Be Done" are mantras.

What constrains the text in these nonhymn forms is not poetic meter and rhyme but the musical format and the melodic line. Because these songs are not locked into hymnic structure they tend to be freer in content and more adaptive in use. The thought of one verse does not need to flow into the thought of the next, nor do the verses as a whole need to unfold a single concept or narrative. One can pick and choose verses to fit a given liturgical moment or occasion without doing disservice to the song itself.

As subcategories, each of these forms places a different kind of demand on those singing. Hymns demand recognizing words, interpreting poetic imagery, and paying attention to the development of an idea or narrative. Mantras and ostinatos call for surrender to a chantlike state where words become secondary to the rhythm of repetitive sung prayer. Call-response forms necessitate listening to others and honoring collaborative roles. Multilingual songs require willingness to stretch beyond familiar language patterns to embrace a wider faith community. Verse-refrain forms call for balancing two forms of participation, singing and listening, and honoring both as consciously active.

Much needs to be considered when selecting hymns and songs for liturgical use. Which forms, for example, best lead a given local assembly into liturgical presence and participation? Which forms function best for which processions? When do the hymns and songs in a given celebration support the ritual, and when do they interfere with it? There is no single, simple answer to any of these questions. As *Music in Catholic Worship* has taught us we must apply a mix of musical, liturgical, and pastoral judgments in our decision making. Nonetheless, we can suggest guidelines which will facilitate dealing with these questions. Our starting point is to identify the role of these hymns and songs within the rite.

## Role of Hymns and Songs

**Ritual catalyst.** Christian traditions vary in their use of hymns and songs according to the way each understands its worship service. In those traditions for which the Sunday gathering is primarily a word service, a hymn may serve a didactic purpose, or an evangelistic one, or may act to prod interior conversion. It may be a commentary on the Scripture readings, or a response to the sermon. In such traditions, a hymn functions *as a text* (hence, the importance of singing all of its verses). The hymn is a constitutive element of the worship service *as a hymn*.

The Roman Catholic Sunday worship service, however, is the Mass where the Liturgy of the Word flows toward and is completed in the Liturgy of the Eucharist. What we celebrate is not a devotional service, nor a word service, but a liturgical rite through which we ritually enact the paschal mystery. It is this ritual enactment of the paschal mystery which is primary. The structure, the flow, and the rhythm of the rite all interact for the purpose of allowing this enactment to take place.

Understanding our liturgy as ritual enactment of the paschal mystery explains why the acclamations which punctuate the rite at specific key moments are the most important musical elements in our celebration. This understanding also clarifies the function of hymns and songs. We sing them at the processional moments in the Mass—the Entrance, the Presentation of Gifts, and Communion—where they function not primarily as texts (although their texts are very important) but as *ritual catalysts* for the deeper movement which is occurring within the rite.

**Processional function.** Each procession and its music—Entrance, Presentation of the Gifts, and Communion—has a specific function within the overall rite. The Entrance Song is to prepare us for liturgical celebration by drawing us to deeper unity, leading us into the mystery of the season or feast, and preparing us to hear the Word and celebrate the Eucharist (GIRM §47, *MCW* §§44, 61). Whatever its style or form, the Entrance Song is meant to draw us into liturgical presence and ready us for liturgical participation. Its function is clearly liturgical and not devotional.

The function of the hymn or song during the Presentation of the Gifts is to accompany the procession with the gifts and to make the communal nature of this procession more evident (GIRM §74, *MCW* §71). The function of the music, then, is to support our communal movement toward the deeper self-offering symbolized by the placing of bread and wine on the altar and the offering of gifts for the needy. As the Entrance Song is preparation for the proclamation of the Word so the Presentation song is preparation for the proclamation of the Eucharistic Prayer in which we fully offer ourselves with Christ.

The Communion song is meant to give outward expression to our inward unity in Christ, to express joy for the mystery being celebrated, and to highlight the communal nature of the procession (GIRM §86, *MCW* §62). This means the song is itself sacramental. It both celebrates our communion and assists it to happen. The song expresses the joy we experience in being called to the messianic table to feast on the Body and Blood of

Jesus and to become that Body for one another and the world. The song directs attention outward toward communal celebration rather than inward toward private prayer. Finally, the song supports the processional movement to and from the eucharistic table by intensifying its meaning. Together everyone processes to the messianic table where we celebrate the fullness of our union and redemption in Christ. Our singing as we process is already celebration of this union and this redemption.

While it is common custom to sing a recessional hymn at the close of Mass, and while the forward to the 1985 Sacramentary states that the recession "may be accompanied by a recessional song or other music," this hymn is not actually part of the rite. The real conclusion of the Mass comes with the words of dismissal—e.g., *Go in the peace of Christ*—to which the assembly responds, *Thanks be to God*. As the Sacramentary indicates, the purpose of this dismissal is to "[send] each member of the congregation to do good works, praising and blessing the Lord." The point is to get moving, to return to the ministry of everyday Christian living. It is not necessary, then, and is perhaps even misleading, to sing a closing hymn which keeps us standing in place. A more appropriate way to end would be to accompany our exit back into ordinary time and space with an organ or choir postlude, or simply to allow the sound of our footsteps journeying toward the needs of the world to go unaccompanied.

Analysis reveals that the processional hymns and songs provide an external framework which moves us into and through the structure of the rite. Each one of the processions and the singing which accompanies it moves us to deeper involvement in the rite. The Entrance Song prepares us to hear the Word, the Presentation song draws us to the altar of self-offering, and the Communion song celebrates the completion of our union with Christ and one another. As processional music, then, hymns and songs facilitate our movement to deeper presence.

The analysis also reveals that these hymns and songs function as agents of change. They budge us from one position to another, keeping us moving through the rite's changing structures and demands. Specifically, the Entrance hymn moves us from the "door" of the liturgy to its heart. Through our singing we accompany the ministers from the doorway of the church to the sanctuary space. On a spiritual level we journey from ordinary time and space to liturgical time and space. We move ourselves into the center of the liturgical action. We enter the ritual. In essence we move forward in order to express our willingness to surrender to the action which is about to take place: our transformation into the Body of Christ.

The procession with the gifts is a practical procession: we need to carry the bread and wine to the table to prepare them for the Liturgy of the Eucharist. Also brought forward can be gifts for the poor, in the form of food and money collected, to be given to those in need. What is the spiritual journey symbolized in this procession? It is two-pronged: one movement is the internalization of the message of the Gospel just proclaimed; the other is the final preparation of ourselves for transformation, a sort of "leaning forward" in our seats as we get ready to stand for the dialogue which begins the Eucharistic Prayer.

The procession during Communion is a movement toward completion: We journey to the messianic banquet where we become one in the Body of Christ. We arrive at our destination. We are on the mountaintop, no longer climbing. Here at last we find food for all, love for all, healing for all.

Processional hymns understood in this way function during the rite to move us forward ritually. The Entrance hymn assists us to enter the liturgical action, to let go of all the "busy-ness" of daily living which clings to heart and mind, and blocks our attentive participation in the ritual. The music at the presentation of the gifts helps us traverse from Liturgy of the Word to Liturgy of the Eucharist by helping us to internalize the Word just heard and to ready ourselves for the Eucharistic Prayer which is to come. The Communion hymn celebrates our joyful completeness in and as the Body of Christ. At the conclusion of Mass we do not linger, but get a move on and return— refreshed, restored, fed—to our work of ministry for the salvation of the world.

**A pastoral example.** I once celebrated Sunday Eucharist with a community that comprehended well the ritual function of the hymns. Musicians and ministers clearly understood the rhythm of the rite as it moved from the Entrance to the Concluding Rites and the function of the hymns at different points along the way. The opening hymn was a song of praise in a strong 4.4 meter. The assembly turned to face the ministers as they processed, thereby expressing their sense of moving forward with them into the ritual action. The ministers did not rush down the aisle, but adopted a pace which allowed the assembly time to move with them psychologically. They paced their movement to last the length of the hymn, leaving only the final verse to be sung after the presider reached his place.

The hymn during the Presentation of the Gifts used a text which was based upon the Gospel reading of that day. Verses one and two were sung by choir alone, three and four by the assembly. At the fourth and final verse the cantor gestured the assembly to stand, an action which made it strikingly clear that the hymn had not been simply an activity to keep them occupied while the altar was readied and the collection taken up. Rather, the hymn was integral to their preparation of themselves for the Eucharistic Prayer which was to come. They were the gifts being prepared.

During Communion the music selected was a text with refrain, sung responsorially between choir and assembly. Between verses by choir and refrain by assembly, the organist improvised short interludes to extend the length of the song. Thus there was a seamlessness to the music of the Communion procession with neither assembly nor choir becoming tired by the tedium of too much repetitive singing. At the conclusion of the Communion procession, the assembly stood and sang a hymn of thanksgiving. Their manner of singing was full-throated and joyous, and it was clear that they were celebrating together their having been fed and filled at the messianic banquet. The Communion Rite concluded with the prayer after Communion, and the celebration moved immediately to the final blessing and dismissal. The assembly exited to an energetic organ postlude.

In this celebration the processional hymns were used in such a way that they pulled the assembly into and through the rite.

The rite was understood as an unfolding enactment from the Entrance to the Concluding Rites and its rhythm was allowed to emerge. The processional hymns functioned as the catalysts which moved the ritual forward and drew the people into this movement.

## Guidelines and Principles
## Governing Use of Hymns and Songs

**Honor the function of a procession.** Deciding what hymn or song to use must be determined first of all by the function of the procession under consideration. Because the Entrance Procession is meant to pull the assembly into ritual presence and prepare them for encounter with Christ in the Word, the hymn or song which accompanies it needs to have a strong meter. It needs a text which in some way acknowledges God and God's action, or relates to the feast or season being celebrated, or refers directly to the Gospel about to be proclaimed.

How long should this song be? Its length depends on how long it takes an assembly on a given Sunday to become liturgically present. The length of the hymn or song, then, will vary from assembly to assembly, and from week to week even with the same assembly. Songs in free form facilitate this variableness because their length can be readily adjusted to meet the needs of a given day. Hymns need special consideration, however, because their narrative structure must be honored. One way to honor it is to adjust the timing of the procession by asking the ministers not to begin moving into the space until the second or third verse of the hymn.

The procession with the gifts expresses the assembly's movement toward deeper self-gift. The journey embodied by this procession can be accompanied by silence, by instrumental music alone, by a choir piece, or by an assembly song. Since a different kind of "movement" is going on the music used need not be as energetic as that used for the Entrance procession. It can be strongly metered and strophic or it can be more meditative (in the style of Taizé, for example). Its text may reiterate the message of the Gospel reading, relate to the liturgical feast or season, or simply sing God's praise. Whatever the music chosen, however, neither style nor text should entice the assembly to drift off into private devotional prayer or become distracted by the musical prowess of the choir, soloist, or instrumentalist. The music must keep them focused on the liturgical action which is unfolding.

The Communion procession celebrates the assembly's arrival at the messianic table and the completion of their union and redemption in Christ. The nature of this procession calls for a hymn or song with a gentler style than that of the Entrance Song. And it calls for a text which speaks of the joy of salvation, or of the fullness of being fed by Christ's Body and Blood, or of the sense of union with one another in the messianic banquet. Since this song is to direct our attention outward toward communal celebration rather than inward toward private prayer, hymns which speak of adoration of the Blessed Sacrament—hymns proper to Benediction and to times of eucharistic adoration—are not appropriate during the Communion Rite. Finally, because this song is an outward expression of inward unity in Christ (GIRM §86) it is never to be lightly omitted, either by the music planners or by an individual member of the assembly who chooses not to sing. For the planners this means choosing songs which the assembly can sing easily and well. For the assembly members this means choosing to enter into the communal singing even when the song is somewhat unfamiliar, or not to one's liking, or a distraction from private prayer. It means entering in with full heart and letting the community's common voice carry one's singular struggling voice. It means entering in with full heart and letting the text of the song transform one's private prayer into the shared prayer of the Body of Christ.

This is the one procession in which every member of the assembly physically participates. The procession is symbolic of what is taking place: everyone, the able and the lame, the ready and the not-so-ready, the healed and those in need of healing, processes to the messianic table in celebration of their redemption in Christ. Walking forward to the Lord's table and walking together are both very important. So is the communal singing which accompanies this movement. This leads to two issues which need addressing. The first is the logistical problem of walking, singing, carrying a book, and receiving the eucharistic bread and cup all at the same time. One way to resolve this problem is to begin the Communion music instrumentally and improvise until enough people have returned to their places to carry the singing. Another way is to use responsorial forms of music which free the assembly from having to carry books (and frees them to watch one another moving in procession). A third resolution is to pare the repertoire of Communion songs down to a small number of well-selected pieces which the assembly can eventually sing by heart.

The second issue raised by the importance of having everyone process to the messianic table has to do with when and how the choir and those leading the music are to process. Since the song is to begin when the presider gives himself Communion (GIRM §159) the choir and the musicians are occupied at the beginning of the procession. Logistics of their participation in the procession must be worked out in a way that is practical yet still symbolically and sacramentally complete. Each church space and each situation will require its own resolution. The best I have experienced was a parish where the assembly stood for the entire Communion procession until everyone had received. The choir processed at the end of the line while the music director improvised at the keyboard. Finally, she processed up to receive. The continued standing of the assembly while she received communicated their unity with her. (The worst I have ever experienced, on the other hand, was watching a eucharistic minister who belonged to a choir reach under his seat at Communion time, pull out a ciborium of preconsecrated hosts, and distribute these to the choir—a liturgical contradiction on every level!)

GIRM (§88) directs that after Communion the assembly may spend some time in silent prayer or they may sing a psalm or hymn. The singing of a post-Communion song is meant to enhance the assembly's sense of Eucharist as a communal act. What is called for is an assembly hymn or song rather than a choir or solo "communion meditation." Having completed the

Communion procession the assembly stands to sing its communal thanksgiving to the One who has called them to this table,
blessed them with nourishment, and transformed them more
fully into Body of Christ. The text sung should not be one which
draws the assembly into private prayer but one which leads
them to communal thanksgiving and praise of God, to celebration of their oneness in Christ, to acknowledgment that they
have been nourished for mission. When a post-Communion
song is sung the Communion song which precedes it should be
concluded in ample time to allow for appropriate transition
(GIRM §86). A good way to handle this would be to finish the
Communion procession with instrumental music only. Furthermore, when singing a hymn of praise after Communion it
would make good ritual sense to omit the recessional hymn.

**Match form to function.** Finally, we must consider the rami-
fications of the musical form itself. Does the form of a given
hymn or song enable the processional action which is meant to
take place? Does it move the assembly forward liturgically, i.e.,
to the Word, to the altar, to the messianic meal? It is this issue
which generates a tenuous relationship between hymn form
and liturgical structure. Because a hymn by definition develops
a narrative or theme over successive strophes it must be given
full scope to deliver its meaning. Its textual demands, which
must be honored, can be at odds with the time frame of a given
procession.

Song forms which are not locked into hymnic structure (i.e.,
verse-refrain pieces, call-response songs, Taizé mantras, for example) are generally freer in both function and content. The
thought of one verse does not need to flow into the thought of
the next, nor do the verses as a whole necessarily unfold a
single concept or narrative. One can choose specific verses to fit
a given procession without doing disservice to the song itself.
Not every song is so adaptable, however. Sometimes the musical structure of a song requires that it be sung in its entirety.
Gerard Chuisano's energetic and uplifting "On This Moun-
tain," for example, is a verse-refrain piece which changes
melody on verse three then segues to verse four without the

intervening refrain. One cannot sing some verses of this song and omit others without destroying its integrity.

In either situation, hymn or song, the integrity of the liturgy and the purpose of the procession must be honored lest the attention of the assembly become sidetracked. When considering any hymn or song for liturgical use we must evaluate all of its components—form, style, tempo, and text—in terms of their ability to support the processional movement.

**Meet the needs of the assembly.** In addition to the purpose of the procession which the hymn or song will accompany we need to consider also the nature and needs of the assembly who will be singing it. The music must be accessible to, meaningful for, and singable by this particular assembly. And here comes the rub. The fact that a piece of music is accessible, meaningful, and singable for a particular assembly does not necessarily mean that it is appropriate for liturgical use. Hymns and songs which express privatized devotion, or serve a catechetical or didactic purpose, or are intended to evangelize the unbelieving interfere with the purpose of liturgy. We need to be discerning in our choices. What hymns and songs will pull this assembly into *liturgical* presence and enable their *liturgical* participation? Which ones make them conscious of their identity as Body of Christ and of the liturgical call to enter ritual enactment of the paschal mystery? Which ones open up the liturgical year's sequential celebration of the mystery of Christ as a source of Christian identity and power?

At the same time it is also true that the most liturgically appropriate, well-written hymn or song can be a stumbling block for a given community. The most beautifully constructed Bach chorale can be the worst liturgical choice for an assembly for whom, for whatever reasons, such music does not speak liturgically. Or the music may be liturgically potent, but performed so poorly that it impedes rather than invites liturgical participation. There are two issues here: what music is in fact liturgical music, and what music helps *this* community enter the liturgical mystery. Answering these questions challenges us to know the rite, to know the nature of liturgy, and to know the culture and character of our local community.

Furthermore, we must add to our discernment process the complexity raised by the multicultural composition of so many of our parishes today. Whatever the cultural makeup, we need to use hymns and songs which the people find accessible as well as introduce ones which will pull them out of and beyond their comfort zones. Our musical choices must be pastorally sensitive and culturally responsive as well as liturgically sound.

Finally, one of the roles of hymns and songs, which are diverse and variable, is to stand in balanced relationship with musical elements in the liturgy which are relatively unchanging. Consistent elements such as the eucharistic acclamations ground the assembly in the ritual repetition needed for deepening their identity as the baptized community of the Church. Changing elements such as hymns and songs, on the other hand, provide the impetus to stretch that identity to new boundaries. When are the hymns and songs we sing meeting this challenge, and when are they failing to meet it? They miss the mark when they change so much that they pull the attention of the assembly to themselves rather than to the core of the ritual. They also miss the mark when they change so little that the liturgy becomes perfunctory and the participation of the assembly flaccid. A good rule of thumb is to look over the entire liturgical year and select three or four new pieces to introduce to the assembly. Spread the introduction of each one out over a period of time. Begin with a note in the parish bulletin about its style, content, language, and liturgical appropriateness. Use it as an instrumental and/or choral prelude for a few weeks before teaching it to the assembly. Then let the assembly sing it over a long enough period of time for them to integrate it effectively into their repertoire.

## Notes

[1] Cited in Edward Foley, *From Age to Age: How Christians Have Celebrated the Eucharist* (Chicago: Liturgy Training Publications, 1991) 52.

[2] Austin Lovelace, *The Anatomy of Hymnody* (Chicago: GIA Publications, 1965) 5.

# Singing the Responsorial Psalm

In my early years as a music director I used to described the role of the responsorial Psalm in the words of *Music in Catholic Worship*: "this unique and very important song is the response to the first lesson" (§63). In recent years, however, I have come to find this definition is too limiting. If, as the General Instruction of the Roman Missal indicates, the psalm is indeed "an integral part of the liturgy of the word" (§61) standing as "an independent rite or act" (§37) then its function in relation to the Liturgy of the Word must be much broader than we have given credit.

This chapter begins by exploring the role of the responsorial Psalm as response to the entire Liturgy of the Word and as bridge between first reading and Gospel. It then outlines some liturgical and pastoral principles for selecting responsorial Psalm settings and for implementing the singing of the psalm.

## A Broader Role for the Responsorial Psalm

**New perspective.** In an essay published at the time of the promulgation of the 1970 Lectionary, Peter Purdue stated that although the responsorial Psalm is intentionally related to the first reading by similarity of text, content, or mood, it is not a response to the Old Testament reading but *"the* response of the people to the word of God they hear in all three readings."[1] Purdue based his argument on the fact that a chain of relationship runs from the first reading through the Psalm to the Gospel. The first reading was chosen to be proclaimed with this Gospel either because it contained some thematic resemblance, or provided some contrast, or presented some Old Testament background, or projected some prophetic foreshadowing. The verses of the psalm were then deliberately selected to relate to the first reading. When we read the first reading, Psalm and Gospel of a given Sunday as an integrated set, this relationship becomes evident (outside of the festal seasons of Advent, Christmas, Lent, and Easter and the solemnities such as the Assumption, the Nativity of John the Baptist, and SS. Peter and Paul, etc., the second reading is not connected to the other two, but runs along its own track). According to Purdue when we sing the responsorial Psalm we are responding to the Gospel as well as to the first reading.

Jean-Pierre Prévost, former professor of Old Testament and Hebrew at St. Paul University, Ottawa, once said that the role of the responsorial Psalm is to act as the bridge between the first reading and the Gospel. This image accords with the principle in the Lectionary that the end point or climax of the Liturgy of the Word is the Gospel reading for which the preceding elements prepare us (Introduction to the Lectionary, §13). The image of responsorial Psalm as bridge conveys a dual sense of both movement and connectedness. The movement aspect of the metaphor implies that we begin the Liturgy of the Word in one place and cross over to another. There is a journey here. Where does it begin? Where does it end? Where are we—spiritually, mentally, emotionally, liturgically—at the start of the Liturgy of the Word? Where are we at its end? and How do we get there? The connectedness aspect of the figure of speech communicates that the beginning and the ending of this journey are related, that our starting point and our ending point form adjoining shorelines. What we cross over in between varies at different times during the liturgical year. At times it is moving water or a field ripe with grain, and at other times it is a dry gulch or even a frighteningly deep canyon.

What is the passing-over that we undertake? The movement is not a journey through time, that is, from the Old Testament period to that of the Gospel, but a journey of transformation. We begin the Liturgy of the Word standing on the threshold of one way of being; we cross over to new self-understanding as Body of Christ. Prévost is suggesting that the bridge which carries us to this new way of being is the text of the responsorial Psalm.

The movement within the psalm text itself, its internal changes of mood, of focus, of content, and of image, indicates the movement that is meant to take place within us. A relationship exists between the internal movement expressed in the psalm—the process of transformation and conversion within the heart, mind, and behavior of the psalmist—and the liturgical assembly praying that psalm within the context of the Liturgy of the Word. And singing the psalm in responsorial fashion is directly related to the manner in which the transformation takes place. As we listen to the cantor's voice unfold the story of the psalm, we respond with increasing recognition and surrender.

A third notion about the role of the responsorial Psalm comes from Irene Nowell, Scripture scholar and author of *Sing a New Song: The Responsorial Psalms in the Sunday Lectionary.*[2] Stimulated by Ralph Kiefer's comment that "the Responsorial Psalm constitutes a summation of the word for that day,"[3] Nowell carefully studied each psalm in the Sunday Lectionary in relation to the set of readings in the Lectionary to which it was assigned. Investigating the juxtaposition of a particular psalm with a particular set of readings generated new meanings and connections within the Liturgy of the Word. Going further than either Purdue or Prévost, Nowell uses the frame of the psalm to relate the second reading to the other two, a connection generally difficult to achieve outside of the festive seasons.

For Nowell the responsorial Psalm is the avenue not only to understanding the whole of the Liturgy of the Word but also to appropriating its meaning for our lives. Because the psalms are poetry they move us beyond the hearing of a discursive text to participation in that text as personal experience. The responsorial Psalm is the key that unlocks the meaning of the Liturgy of the Word and the doorway by which we internalize that meaning.

All three writers coincide in their sense that the responsorial Psalm is more than just response to the first reading. Purdue shows how the psalm is response to the Liturgy of the Word as a whole. Prévost suggests that the psalm is more than response, it is the bridge we cross over into the transformation to which the Gospel calls us. And Nowell demonstrates that the psalm does in fact bring this transformation about.

**Applying this perspective.** In this section I apply this broader concept of the role of the responsorial Psalm to two specific sets of readings. My first goal here is to show how the primary ministers of music—the assembly—can and ought to use the psalm to open up their understanding of the readings of the day. My secondary goal is to suggest how the cantor as music minister is to embody that understanding in the manner in which she sings the psalm.

The first example is from the Fifteenth Sunday of Ordinary Time, Year A. In the first reading (Isa 55:10-11) we find Isaiah comparing God's word to the rain and snow that come down from heaven. Both inevitably accomplish the purpose for which they are sent. There is power here, and it is the indomitable power of God. Yet the Gospel reading contradicts the assertion of Isaiah. In the parable of the sower and the seed (Matt 13:1-23) we hear that God's word does not always achieve its goal, for human sinfulness can block the power of the word. The two readings stand opposite each other: God's plan, which is always fulfilled, is blocked by the circumstances of human living and the choices of human beings.

What bridges the contradiction between these two readings is the confidence of Psalm 65. In it we sing that God has prepared both the grain and the land, "softening it with showers, / blessing its yield."[4] The effect of the psalm is to turn our attention to the God who waters and plants. We must be honest about the resistance to God's word that the Gospel tells us is ever present within the world and within our own hearts, but we need not lose hope because of it. The key is to focus our attention on the graciousness of God rather than on our own ungraciousness.

How wonderful, the psalm says, that God persists in visiting the "land" of our hearts and working it until we yield to receiving what God desires to plant. How wonderful that the word of God is stronger than any resistance we or the world put up against it. No matter that we are slow to receive the seed, reticent to let it grow, distracted from the task, God will bring what has been planted to abundant harvest. The psalm invites us, with all the fields and valleys, to sing and shout for joy!

The cantor's ministry in singing this psalm is to communicate the assurance that no ground, no matter how poor, is left untilled by God. Whatever dry clods are in the way of our receiving God's word and letting it grow, God will tend to. We have only to let God do this work. The cantor needs to embody this surrender physically and emotionally. Her tone of voice, facial expression, body stance, and gesture need to express that unbroken confidence in God that comes from surrendering oneself to God's word. The cantor needs to let herself blossom before the eyes of the assembly so that they can see in her earthiness the fruitfulness that is being born there.

The second example shows how the psalm bridges the first reading and Gospel on the Twenty-sixth Sunday of Ordinary Time, Year A. In the first reading Ezekiel points out that it is not God who chooses the death of the wicked, but the wicked themselves (Ezek 18:25-28). Those who turn from wickedness save their lives. Yet the chief priests and elders in the Gospel (Matt 21:23-32) persist in choosing death by acting like the lazy son who pays lip service to doing his father's bidding but never follows through on his promise of obedience. Here we have the possibility of change juxtaposed with the refusal to be changed. Salvation has been promised and is possible, but it is not easy.

Again, the psalm turns our attention to the goodness of God who "shows sinners the way" and "guides the humble to justice" (Ps 25). The first reading and Gospel point out that we have a tenuous hold on righteousness and easily fluctuate between "yes" and "no" to God. But the psalm indicates that God is a forgiving savior who never wavers. The psalmist even sneakily reminds God of this by alluding to the "little creed" ("The LORD, the LORD, a merciful and gracious God, slow to anger and rich in kindness and fidelity" [Exod 34:6] was a phrase first spoken not *about* God but *by* God as direct revelation to Moses: this is my name—Lord—and this is who I am—merciful, gracious, compassionate. The phrase appears so often in the Old Testament that it is called the "little creed," a capsule profession of who God is and how God relates to humankind). God will teach us all we need to know and to live rightly and God will forgive us when we fail. We have only to ask, and to be honest (humble) about ourselves.

In singing this psalm the cantor needs to let her or his body express the humility that arises out of honest self-knowledge and unwavering confidence in God's guidance and mercy. How does one stand before the assembly with such humility yet poise? The key is for the cantor to use the psalm as a means of personal encounter with God. How does this psalm invite the cantor to relate to God? What "ways" does the cantor need to ask God to teach her or him? A cantor who makes such prayer part of personal preparation will communicate more than the words of the psalm to the assembly when the psalm is sung. The cantor will communicate the personal transformation that God is working within the heart.

Two important things are evident from the above analyses. The first is what the psalm does: in addition to bridging the first reading and Gospel the psalm keeps our attention focused on God. The hearing of the Word and the singing of the responsorial Psalm are meant to be a continuous act of worship, one that will be completed in our coming to the messianic table of Christ's Body and Blood. The second is that the body gestures of the cantor are meant to communicate far more than just a cue about when to sing the refrain. What the cantor is communicating above all is this act of worship, this continuous focusing on God. However intensely a given psalm expresses human feeling, the purpose of this expression is never for the sake of the feeling itself, but always for praise of and surrender to the One who understands all feeling.

These examples of using the psalm to enter into and respond to the whole of the Liturgy of the Word reinforce the argument for its broader role. Through our reflection on the psalm we gain greater insight into the readings and deepen our participation in the proclamation of the Word. For the assembly the psalm is a bridge to transformation. For the cantor the psalm is an invitation to lead the way across.

The above discussion presents a more developed schema for understanding the role of the responsorial Psalm than we have previously envisioned. As with other elements of its reform, many of the liturgical revisions of Vatican II were only seed plantings. Our faithful practicing of these reforms is bringing these seedlings to maturity, and in this case the fruit is turning out to be far juicier and more nutritious that we had expected.

## Some Liturgical and Pastoral Principles

**Selecting musical settings.** The overriding purpose of the responsorial Psalm is to assist the gathered Church to surrender to the paschal mystery, particularly as that is being played out in the Liturgy of the Word. The Word issues a prophetic challenge that we, the gathered Church, be true to the ideal which stands before us, that is, to be in our own lives the dying and rising Christ. The Word confronts us with how far we fall short of that identity and mission, as well as with how continuously God (the Trinity) forgives our failings and faithfully supports us to continue growing in our surrender. The Word reminds us of our ideal selves, of our identity as Body of Christ, of our mission to heal the sick, to feed the hungry, to clothe the naked, and to forgive one another.

What we experience in the proclamation of Scripture is a continuously new encounter with the reality of God's faithfulness, and with the ideal of faithfulness to which we are summoned in response. With Christ we are called to surrender to the paschal mystery. When we sing the responsorial Psalm we express that surrender in word and voice. The cantor leads the surrender, embodying it in breath and melody, and mirroring through her gesture the dialogue which is taking place between Christ and his assembled Church. When we the assembly respond we sacramentalize our assent, that is we make our surrender audibly, visibly, physically apparent. In other words, we are doing far more in the responsorial Psalm than merely singing a song. We are saying yes to the ideal that is being placed before us, and that ideal is not a set of directives, but a living, breathing relationship. And to stay in that relationship we must assent to our own death and resurrection. When we select a musical setting of a responsorial Psalm what needs to be considered above all is the extent to which it is capable of supporting this act of surrender. The music must open up both the text of the psalm and the hearts of the assembly.

Because the psalm is a liturgical text, the text given in the Lectionary is preferable to a paraphrased version. Although the psalm is not proclamation, it is a scriptural text which bears direct relation to the readings of the day. While it is true that even the translations in the Lectionary are paraphrases to some extent—since adapting concepts from one language to another always requires adjustments—there is a huge difference between a translation that is exegetically based and a paraphrase that is determined by the requirements of a melodic line. There are many highly paraphrased psalm texts available which are poetically beautiful and musically uplifting, but these function more appropriately at other times in the liturgy (for example, during the Communion procession). The issue here is not the quality of the music but the capability of the psalm setting to fulfill its specific liturgical role.

A second principle in selecting a psalm setting is that the text of the psalm must predominate over the music. If the music is so elaborate, or so thickly woven either chorally or instrumentally that the text cannot be readily heard and understood, then the setting cannot fulfill the role of the responsorial Psalm. This is not to say that the music cannot be rhythmically or harmonically complex, but only that the complexity should not overshadow the clarity of the words. How often people leave the Sunday Eucharist humming the melody of the psalm refrain, but do they also know what psalm was sung, and how that psalm was related to the readings of the day?

Adjunct to this principle is the principle that the psalm never overshadow the readings themselves. If the setting is so long or so embellished that the assembly continues mentally humming the refrain during the subsequent readings, then the psalm has overreached its place. This is a difficult principle to implement for the psalm, and the manner in which it is presented, must be inviting in order for it to lead the assembly to respond. What we need to keep in front of our vision is that the psalm is meant to lead us to the readings not to itself. (Unfortunately, the problem which often exists is not that the psalm setting is too elaborate, but that the proclamation of the readings is too weak. The need, then, is not to tone down the psalm but to improve the proclamation.)

This is not to say that we never use an elaborate musical setting of a responsorial Psalm. This is more than appropriate on solemnities like Christmas, Easter, Christ the King, etc. On these occasions highly embellished musical settings—with perhaps more than one cantor or the choir as a whole singing the verses in harmony, and with solo instrument(s) added—communicate the high festivity of the day in contrast with the less festive periods of the year. These solemnities call for more elaborate music. But highly ornamented psalm settings lose their festive capability if they are used on a regular basis, Sunday after Sunday.

**Helping the assembly.** One means of leading the assembly to fuller participation in the responsorial Psalm is to print the upcoming Sunday psalm refrain in the same spot in the bulletin each week. This "spotlight" could include an invitation to make the refrain a prayer mantra throughout the week. It could also include one or two sentences about the relationship of the psalm to the readings of the day. An excellent resource in this regard is the short commentary I write each week on "Appreciating the Responsorial Psalm" in *Living Liturgy: Spirituality, Celebration, and Catechesis for Sundays and Solemnities.*[5] Another excellent resource is *Sing a New Song* by Irene Nowell, cited above.

A second—and essential—aid is to select psalm settings that are easily singable, both for the cantor and for the assembly. This norm will be relative to the abilities of your cantor(s) and your assembly. What is the singing capability of your assembly? How used to singing the responsorial Psalm are they? If watching and listening to a cantor is new to them, begin with simpler musical settings until their sung response becomes automatic.

If the practice of singing the responsorial Psalm is new for your parish, the most important starting point will be to use a confident and competent cantor. This may mean having the same cantor sing every week at a given Mass for several months, while other cantors are in training. The goal is to allow the assembly time to become comfortable and secure with responding to a cantor, and this is easier for them to do when the cantor in front of them is both familiar and competent. Remember, the goal is not to involve as many people as possible in the ministry of cantor, but to lead the assembly toward their participation in the singing of the psalm refrain.

It might be helpful during this period of becoming accustomed to singing the responsorial Psalm to use seasonal psalm refrains so that the people are not having to learn new music every week. The Lectionary lists the texts of seasonal psalms and refrains in nos. 173–74. One of the most valuable outcomes of this approach in the beginning stages of introducing responsorial psalmody is that the people will learn to look at the cantor rather than following a line of music in the hymnal, missal, or worship aid. The same principle we use with the proclamation of the readings applies here. Our goal is to lead the assembly to look at and listen to the cantor rather than to follow along in a book. In this way the singing of the responsorial Psalm will become the dialogue it is meant to be.

Whether the members of the assembly are novices or veterans with singing the responsorial Psalm, it is important that the cantor be attentive to them. It must be obvious that the cantor's concern is focused on them rather than caught up with self. The cantor needs to give the assembly eye contact when the text is addressed to them and to indicate with body and eye posture when the text is addressed to God. This takes time to learn to do well and comfortably. It also requires spending some time analyzing the content of the text.

**Helping the cantor.** In terms of your cantor(s), what a skillful cantor may sing well a less trained or experienced one may not. This means that psalm settings need to be chosen with specific cantors in mind, and adaptations need to be made. For example, with a given refrain two different settings of the verses might be used, one simplified, the other more melodically developed. Do not make the mistake, however, of thinking that psalm tones (such as the Gelineau ones, for example) are easier to sing. Their simplicity is deceptive. Because they are text-driven rather than melodically controlled they are in fact more demanding, requiring greater preparation of the text, and greater self-effacement on the part of the cantor who must step aside to let the text shine instead of her own vocal prowess. It is this transparency of the text which makes psalm tones so effective liturgically.

Train all of your cantors, the skillful as well as the less skillful, to prepare the singing of the psalm in the context of the readings. Even before they look at the psalm, have them read the Gospel and the first reading and spend some time reflecting on and praying over them. Then have them look at the text of the psalm and see how it is connected to the readings. The best pastoral resource for helping cantors do this is *Living Liturgy*, cited above, which is published annually by the Liturgical Press. This resource contains the readings and psalm for each Sunday and solemnity of the liturgical year, offers a reflection on how the Gospel invites us to paschal mystery living, and provides insight into how the responsorial Psalm of the day enables us to better understand and enter into the Liturgy of the Word. The book also suggests an area of cantor spirituality appropro to the psalm and intended to guide the cantor's lived preparation during the week prior to singing the psalm.

I have personally found this to be the best cantor preparation that I can do. Once I have a sense of how the psalm is connected to the readings, I have a better sense of how to sing it. I develop a new understanding of the psalm and of how I need to phrase it. I realize that I am singing more than the text of the psalm, that my singing is actually a dialogue with the readings which mirrors the dialogue going on between God and the assembly in the Liturgy of the Word. A dimension emerges that is deeper than the music alone, and that same dimension begins to open up within me. When I finally sing the psalm, what I am singing is not notes, but this deeper dimension, which is nothing less than the working of God leading me to surrender to the Word.

And it is this which the assembly hears, this to which they respond.

## Notes

[1] Peter Purdue, "The New Lectionary," *Doctrine and Life* 19 (1969) 666–79.

[2] Irene Nowell, *Sing a New Song: The Psalms in the Sunday Lectionary* (Collegeville, Minn.: The Liturgical Press, 1993).

[3] Ralph Kiefer, *To Hear and to Proclaim: Introduction, Lectionary for Mass with Commentary for Musicians and Priests* (Washington, D.C.: The Pastoral Press, 1983) 81.

[4] This and subsequent citations from the responsorial Psalms are taken from the 1998 Lectionary for Mass.

[5] Joyce Ann Zimmerman, C.PP.S, and others, *Living Liturgy: Spirituality, Celebration, and Catechesis for Sundays and Solemnities* (Collegeville: The Liturgical Press). This resource is published annually to coincide with the liturgical year.

# Singing the Litanies

This chapter examines the litanies within the eucharistic rite: the *Kyrie,* the General Intercessions, and the *Lamb of God.* What prayer forms are these? What spirituality does each engender? Should they be sung and, if so, how? Answering these questions is not as easy as one might initially expect for each of these prayers has a convoluted history, each frequently suffers from being misunderstood in terms of its content and purpose, and the intercessions, though litanic in origin, are no longer litanic in style. Basically, we would do well to enhance the role of the *Kyrie* and the *Lamb of God* without at the same time inadvertently exaggerating their role in the liturgy. We also need to deepen our understanding of the General Intercessions so that they more effectively carry their intended power in the rite.

This chapter begins by exploring the nature of litanic prayer. The chapter continues in the chronological order in which the three litanies appear in the Mass, sharing a little bit of the history of each and exploring some ways we might better understand their nature and purpose. Finally, the chapter reflects on the kind of spirituality each inculcates and suggest ways to pray them better. Some of these ways are sung, some are not.

## The Form and Effect of Litanic Prayer

Whether prayed as part of a devotional service or a liturgical celebration the form of a litany remains the same. The content is usually intercessory (although litanies of praise and thanks-giving do exist). The form is a pattern of short variable invocations or petitions followed by a short invariable response. The invocations are usually stated or sung by a single person or small group (such as a schola or choir) and the response made by the entire community.

Because of the shortness of both the invocations and the response when we pray a litany we enter into a mantra-like state set up by the rhythm of call and response going on between the leader(s) and the group. The litany draws us into a pattern of communal, rhythmic breathing. What we breath together is the intercessory prayer. In fact, it is this quiet, communal breathing which is the prayer. In our shared rhythmic breathing we inhale all of our human life and exhale all of our need that this life be blessed, healed, sanctified, protected, etc. The very nature of litanic prayer is one of quiet presence to God and to one another as we breathe in our shared humanity and breathe out our shared hope in the mercy and goodness of God who loves that humanity and grants it wholeness.

From early times this rhythm of shared breathing and prayer made litanies the ready accompaniments for processions. The rhythm of communal singing and breathing supported the rhythm of communal walking. The short invariable response enabled easy walking by precluding the need to carry anything other than one's own heart. The intercessory content made the procession a paradigm of the entire journey of life with its continual cry for God's protection and beneficence along the way.

While most litanies are intercessory not all intercessory prayer is litanic. My point here is that the rhythm which characterizes a litany—the steady back and forth flow between leader and community, between breath and prayer—does not occur in the same way with, for example, the General Intercessions in the form in which they were restored by Vatican II. In a typical litany such as the Litany of Saints in its traditional chant form, for example, the length of the invocations remains relatively equal even when their content changes. Sing some of this litany and you'll see what I mean: "St. Michael, pray for us; SS. Peter and Paul, pray for us; All holy men and women, pray for us," etc. No matter what the text the rhythm of invocation and response flows with a relatively even pulse. By contrast the General Intercessions lack this kind of steady rhythm. To illustrate, walk across the room singing part of the Litany of Saints, then process back while singing (or reciting) some typical General Intercessions. With the one you will find yourself easily establishing a pace; with the other you will find yourself wanting to halt in order to think about the text. Even with well-constructed, brief, to-the-point intentions the General Intercessions simply do not set up the same kind of rhythm a litany does. In fact, the General Intercessions are better prayed with a halt in the verbalization, that is, with a built-in pause for silent prayer after each announcement of intention (as we have in the intercessions of Good Friday). Prayed this way the intercessions create this pattern: announcement of intention, followed by silent prayer, followed by invitation (for example, *we pray to the Lord*) and communal response (for example, *Lord, hear our prayer*). It becomes clear that the General Intercessions call for a posture of standing in place, of remaining still so that the prayer can pool itself before we raise it up. The posture called for by litany, on the other hand, is procession, movement from one place in life to another accompanied all the while—even when that movement is only symbolic or psychological—by our cries of intercession and blessing.

## Litanies in the Eucharistic Rite

**The *Kyrie*.** As we pray it today the *Kyrie* is a vestige of a longer litany of petitions which served originally in the place of today's restored General Intercessions.[1] By the fourth century it had been adopted from non-Christian worship as the assembly's response to a litany of petitions prayed after the readings and homily. Near the end of the fifth century, for reasons unidentified by scholars, Pope Gelasius I moved this litany to a position within the opening rites. By the eighth century the petitions had disappeared and only the acclamatory response remained in the ninefold format of *Kyrie* three times, *Christe* three times, and again *Kyrie* three times—the format which eventually became fixed as the first element of the sung ordinary of the Mass. During the Middle Ages many local variations added tropes appropriate to the feast of the day, and these in turn became the tags for titling groups of Mass ordinaries (for example, *Missa orbis factor* or *Missa cuntipotens genitor deus*). The Council of Trent eliminated these tropes but Vatican II reinstated them as a variable part of the third option (C) of today's penitential rite.

Thus, in today's liturgy the *Kyrie* litany is attached to the penitential rite, either incorporated into it or prayed as its conclusion. Its effectiveness as a litany, however, is greatly limited because of its brevity. I say this because the power of a litany to induce a rhythm of shared breathing and prayer is directly related to its lengthiness. With the *Kyrie,* however, we are hardly into it before it is over. This very brevity implies a purpose which is different from that of a litany of typical length. Although litanic in form the *Kyrie* functions much more like acclamation. What we have in the *Kyrie* is a brief litany of praise of Christ as Lord and redeemer, a short shout of acclamation for the one who saves from sin and death and leads us to the Kingdom.

Since the major components of the introductory rites are the Entrance procession with its accompanying hymn and the opening collect, the *Kyrie,* per se, is of secondary importance. But its origins as authentic litany (that is, a lengthy prayer of intercession following the Liturgy of the Word), its present function as acclamation, and the nature of litany as apt accompaniment for procession suggest a way of using it which might make the opening rites more effective. What if we accompanied our Entrance procession with a *Kyrie* litany using invocations drawn from the Gospel of the day? What if a cantor (or schola) led the litany from a place within the procession? This would enable the assembly to follow the procession visually as they sung their response and to understand the music and their part in it more clearly as an integral part of the Entrance procession. This would reunite the power of litany with the movement of procession. The *Kyrie* would then function not as a tag onto the act of penance but as a litany of invocation whereby the assembly calls upon Christ to lead them into this celebration of liturgy. (Perhaps this was even what Pope Gelasius had in mind when he moved the *Kyrie* litany to the Introductory Rites?) At the conclusion of the procession the presider would immediately pray the opening collect, and the assembly would seat themselves for the Liturgy of the Word.

What I suggest here is exploratory and perhaps unworkable. But my concern is to detach the *Kyrie* from its present penitential connotation and resurrect its original litanic and processional capabilities. It is a text with a long and honored history whose present placement and form causes it to border on meaninglessness and to interfere with the flow of the Introductory Rites. How can we make better musical and liturgical use of its richness?

**The General Intercessions.** In the early centuries the General Intercessions or "Prayer of the Faithful" followed the Liturgy of the Word (here is where we first find our *Kyrie* litany). Praying for the needs of all humanity was a natural response to having heard the salvific Word of God. The power to lift such prayer was considered a participation in the priesthood of Christ, a right bestowed by baptism. Catechumens were dismissed before these prayers were raised because they did not yet share this right.

The gradual disappearance of the General Intercessions from the Liturgy of the Word is intertwined with the repositioning of the *Kyrie* litany and its eventual reduction to nine responses without invocations, with the demise of liturgy in the language of the people, and with the clericalization of the rite. Although intercessory content appeared elsewhere (for example, in the canon) its form as litany and as prayer of the people remained repressed until the revisions of Vatican II. We have not yet come to full understanding of their meaning and purpose, however. I have already mentioned that they are not really litanic in style, and that their nature calls for moments of silent prayer on the part of the assembly. Some questions to guide our better writing and praying of these intercessions might be: How do these intercessions need to be written and how led so that the community becomes aware of itself as the Body of Christ in prayer for the world? What is their relationship to and difference from pri-

vate intercessory prayer? What kind of evocative language
would lead the assembly to live the Gospel just proclaimed, that
is, to see the relationship between proclamation and mission?

In addition to such questions as these there is the issue of
whether or not the intercessions should be sung. Litanies are
usually sung. But, as I have pointed out, the General Intercessions are not litanic in style. I have often encouraged the singing
of the intercessions, but I do not in fact think singing them is essential to their nature or effectiveness. The important thing is
that their rendering allow for the pooling of a well of communal
prayer which can then be lifted up for the sake of the Church, the
world, the needy, the community. Depending on how the texts
are written, singing them might actually get in the way of the assembly's quiet reception of them. On the other hand, writing
them so that they can be sung might guarantee their brevity and
intelligibility. Perhaps the best norm would be the principle of
progressive solemnity. Sing the intercessions during the Easter
and Christmas seasons and on solemnities such as All Saints and
Christ the King. On all other occasions recite them.

**The *Lamb of God*.** Of Eastern origin the *Lamb of God* litany
was introduced into the Western Rite in the seventh century
during the papacy of Sergius I.[2] This litany accompanied the
fraction rite and was protracted while whole loaves of bread
were broken apart, their pieces placed in linen sacks then car-
ried by acolytes to various ministers for distribution to the
people. When in the eleventh to twelfth centuries the Roman
Rite began using ready-made hosts of unleavened bread, the
fraction rite became greatly minimalized and this litany was re-
duced to only three repetitions sung by the choir alone. Eventually its placement moved to the kiss of peace and its third
response became *grant us peace.* Vatican II restored its place as
accompaniment to the fraction rite and its form as a chant of
the people, and made provision for its lengthening as needed.

We are readily familiar with references to Christ as Lamb of
God, both from John the Baptist's appellation of him as the lamb
who takes away our sins, and from the numerous references in
Revelation to him as the Lamb who sits at the throne of God and

in whose blood we are purified. We are likewise familiar with the scriptural references to ourselves as the lambs whom Christ shepherds and for whom he cares. But are we equally aware that the New Testament also refers to us as sacrificial lambs? We are not only the lambs whom Christ feeds (John 21:15); we are also lambs sent on a mission fraught with danger and the possibility of death (Luke 10:3).[3] This dual application of the image of sacrificial lamb to both Christ and us his disciples throws a powerful slant on our singing of the *Lamb of God* litany during the rite of fracturing. What is being fractured? For whom? Not only Christ for us, but us for the world. We are the bread that is broken, the wine that is poured out. No wonder we intercede for mercy and peace from the Lamb who has first given his life for us.

This tells us that the rite of fracturing is far too significant to be minimalized or to be allowed to slip by unnoticed. Nor should the singing of the *Lamb of God* be minimalized. It is meant to call us to participation in the symbolic gesture of being broken apart and poured out that all may eat and drink. Yet how often do the fraction rite and the *Lamb of God* begin and end with no more than our cursory attention? To what extent do we consider the *Lamb of God* nothing but filler music while we wait for Communion to begin? To what extent do presiders and eucharistic ministers think the breaking of the consecrated bread and the pouring of the consecrated wine are purely functional gestures?

How might our doing of the fraction rite and our singing of the *Lamb of God* be different if we realized the profound symbolic weight these gestures carry? For one thing, we would not begin the fraction and the litany while the assembly was still engaged in sharing the sign of peace. For another the presider would do the fraction with deliberation and make it clearly visible to all. For a third we would select musical settings of the litany which reflect the import of the action it accompanies. This litany needs to be sung with deliberation and grace so that through singing it we come to understand what we are choosing for ourselves in coming to the eucharistic table. In the Lamb of God we have both litanic content and form, we have length and repetitiveness, time to develop a rhythm of shared breathing and prayer, and we need to make use of it. We need to con-sciously connect the *Lamb of God* to the fraction rite, then let both fraction and litany unfold with the solemnity fitting the li-turgical action which is taking place. The procession this litany accompanies is psychological rather than physical, but it is no less important because of that—through it we take the final steps of our internal journey toward the choice for which the liturgy has been preparing us from its beginning: to be the Body of Christ given for the life of the world. Once this choice is made we are ready to begin joyfully our physical procession toward bread and wine, Body and Blood, life and death.

## Concluding Remark

The intent of this chapter has been to develop a clearer under-standing of the meaning and purpose of each of the three lita-nies in the eucharistic rite—the *Kyrie*, the General Intercessions, and the *Lamb of God*—and to explore better ways of praying them. Although these three litanies are of minor importance in the rite, they are nonetheless chants and/or prayers of the people which are also texts of the rite. Without exaggerating their role in such a way that they compete with other, more im-portant, elements of the rite, we do need to enhance our ritual use of them. We need to enable each to emerge appropriately from within its ritual context. To do so will be to enhance the liturgy as a whole.

## Notes

[1] See Robert Cabié, *The Eucharist,* vol. 2, *The Church at Prayer,* ed. A. G. Martimort, rev. ed. (Collegeville, Minn.: The Liturgical Press, 1986) 53–54, 69–75.

[2] Ibid., 110–11.

[3] See Joyce A. Zimmerman, C.PP.S., "Lamb of God," in *The Collegeville Pastoral Dictionary of Biblical Theology,* ed. Carroll Stuhlmueller (College-ville, Minn: The Liturgical Press, 1996) 532.

# Selecting Music with
# the Liturgical Year in Mind

We are conscientious about how our choices on a given Sunday help us engage with the liturgy of that day. We make appropriate choices for the parts of the Mass, and we select hymns that suit the readings given in the Lectionary. But we need to stand back from Sunday as an isolated event and look at our music planning from the perspective of the entire liturgical year. This chapter offers some practical ways to do so. It begins by examining some musical practices that unwittingly impede our entering more fully into the liturgical year. It then suggests some ways we can lead those with whom we share the task of musical leadership (i.e., the choir, folk ensemble, cantors, organists) to a deeper understanding of the relationship between the liturgical year and the music we choose to sing as that year unfolds.

## Unwitting Impediments

As I have evaluated my years of parish music directing I have discovered that oftentimes it was the academic calendar that shaped my musical planning. I was in the habit of giving the choir (and myself) a break during the summer months, partly because we were tired out and partly because many members were absent due to vacations. Once Labor Day rolled around I started rehearsals again. Although I had used the relatively quiet time of summer to plan music for the year, focusing first on Advent and projecting toward the Easter Triduum as the year's climax, I nonetheless found myself jumpstarting the actual work of music ministry somewhere in the middle of Ordinary Time. This necessarily affected both my frame of mind and that of the choir.

For one thing, dropping choir during the summer months gave a misleading message to the parish about the importance of Ordinary Time. It is not "downtime" or "break time" during which we rest from the task of entering into the mystery to which the liturgy calls us. Although "ordinary" can mean "everyday," it does not mean unimportant or inconsequential. On the contrary, the very everydayness of Ordinary Time gives it extraordinary consequence. It constitutes the bulk of our time, and contains the day in and day out choices that shape the deep faithfulness of our lives. In fact, the word "ordinary," in this instance, is related to the word "ordinal," and the word simply means that Ordinary Time is a time when the Sundays are counted—and are not part of a special season. (Cardinal numbers are one, two, three, etc.; ordinal numbers are first, second, third, etc.)

The General Norms for the Liturgical Year and Calendar[1] underscore the importance of Ordinary Time: "Apart from those seasons having their own distinctive character, thirty-three or thirty-four weeks remain in the yearly cycle that do not celebrate a specific aspect of the mystery of Christ. Rather, especially on the Sundays, they are devoted to the mystery of Christ in all its aspects" (§43). What fuller definition of Ordinary Time can be given than to say that it is "devoted to the mystery of Christ in all its aspects"? The definition confronts us with the very paradox that gives Ordinary Time its meaning: that the ordinary can contain the fullness. Although the manner in which we celebrate Ordinary Time must contrast with the more elaborate way in which we celebrate the festal seasons, dropping the choir perhaps leaves the people experiencing Ordinary Time as flat, empty, and unimportant. We need to figure out how we can keep the choir's energy and commitment going through the "ordinary" period, because in doing so, we offer the community a paradigm for what Ordinary

Time is all about: quieter than times of high celebration, yes, but nonetheless consistent in commitment and quality.

A second typical musical practice that truncates our appreciation of the liturgical year is that of shooting our wad at the beginning of a festal season. We tend to construe the first day as the completion of the season. For example, we pull out all the stops for Christmas day and have nothing left for the festal days yet to come. Epiphany falls flat, and often the Baptism of the Lord passes barely acknowledged. If we were to approach the festival as a season, however, we would plan the music accordingly, spreading the musical highlights out to give Epiphany and the Baptism of the Lord their own special embellishment. How much more fully, then, would our communities enter into the fullness of that season and how much more clearly would they understand the shift at its end back to the call of Ordinary Time?

A third practice to examine is that of planning music Sunday by Sunday rather than season by season. When we plan only Sunday by Sunday we miss the forest for the trees, and often fall into the trap of selecting "themes" from the readings around which to choose hymns and choir pieces. We mistakenly set up each Sunday as an end in itself rather than as a point on a continuum.

The solution to this problem is to think seasonally. Begin by spending some time reflecting on each liturgical season as a whole: What is its starting point? What is its conclusion? One very helpful way to discover the meaning of a season and its internal movement is to read in sequence the opening collects (prayers) for each of its Sundays; or, read and reflect on the proper prefaces for each Sunday. These collects and prefaces are watermarks that stamp each season with an identifying character. Prayerful reflection on them can likewise characterize our thinking and open our minds and hearts to new understandings.

Next, survey your parish's repertoire of service music. What settings of the *Alleluia*/Gospel verse and of the eucharistic acclamations seem to express most effectively in style and mood the meaning and the movement of a particular liturgical season? Once you have identified settings that best fit each season, stick with them year in and year out. Over time your parish will come to identify each setting with its respective season, and the music will support their entrance into the movements within the liturgical year. Like the collects and the prefaces, these acclamations will become seasonal watermarks.

## Educating for the Liturgical Year

First, do what is necessary for yourself to grow in our own understanding of the liturgical year. Read and study The General Norms for the Liturgical Year and the Calendar.

Second, select those key points and principles that would be most important for the musical ministers in your parish to understand. For example, do they understand that "through the yearly cycle the Church unfolds the entire mystery of Christ" (§1)? What is the mystery of Christ? A discussion of this question would yield fruitful faith sharing. After this discussion, hang this quote across the front of the choir room so that its import impacts every rehearsal.

Third, talk with these ministers about how the music choices are meant to help the parish community enter into the progression of the liturgical year. In the rehearsal space, hang a chart of the liturgical year with the different seasons clearly identified. During the last weeks of Ordinary Time, before the beginning of the next liturgical year with the First Sunday of Advent, list on the chart the acclamations that will be sung for each season. Let the choir see the whole picture, its progression, and its relatedness to the unfolding mystery of Christ. Discuss with them the reasons for the acclamations selected for each season. For example, when I selected a Howard Hughes *Alleluia*/Gospel verse acclamation found in the *ICEL Resource Collection of Hymns and Service Music for the Liturgy*[2] for the Advent-Christmas season I shared the reasons for my choice with the choir. This acclamation, I explained, has a bell-like quality that exudes joyful expectation. It can be musically embellished during the Christmas weeks by adding bells or tonechimes and singing it in canon. Using it throughout Advent-Christmas will both unify the season and

differentiate between the anticipation of Advent and the fulfillment of Christmas. The choir appreciated this explanation and
entered into learning and leading this acclamation with great
commitment.

At the beginning of each season, talk with the choir about
the meaning of the season and its specific invitation to enter the
mystery of Christ. Then talk with them about the specific progression of the season. For example, show them how the first
two weeks of Advent concentrate on Christ's eschatological
coming at the end of time, and the last two weeks focus on this
coming in the Incarnation. What is the relationship between
these two comings? Show them how Advent and Christmas are
a single season. Teach them about the Christmas progression
from Incarnation, through Epiphany, to the Baptism of the
Lord. Use the opening collects and the prefaces to demonstrate
the progression and the interrelatedness. Finally, add to the
chart the hymns and the choir pieces that will be used during
the season and share with them how the musical choices you
made are intended to help the parish move into and through
this liturgical season.

Taken collectively, the above suggestions are a tall order.
They are not meant to be pursued in a single choir session, or in
a single year. Pick a single starting point and begin. Proceed
slowly—and repeat often. Helping both those in music ministry and the parish as a whole deepen their understanding of the
role of music in relation to the liturgical year will take time, but
it is one of our most important tasks.

## Notes

[1] In *The Liturgy Documents: A Parish Resource* (Chicago: Liturgy Training
Publications, 1991).

[2] *ICEL Resource Collection for Hymns and Service Music for the Liturgy*
(Chicago: GIA Publications, 1981). This collection contains hymns in the
public domain as well as original settings of service music which may be
reproduced without charge for use in parishes, schools, and other similar
groups.

# Selecting Seasonal Sets
# of Service Music

This chapter outlines a process for selecting sets of service music appropriate to each liturgical season, beginning with the rationale for doing so and the principles which should guide the choices involved, and concluding with some suggestions. The goal is to establish seasonal sets of service music which stay in place, that is, which are reserved for the specific liturgical seasons for which they have been selected. Just as changes in art and environment cue the assembly about the changing of the seasons, so must the service music assist the parish to enter into the character of each season and into the unfolding rhythms of the liturgical year. In order for this to happen, the parish needs to have a set of service music in place for each season which has, over time, become recognizable as a characteristic element of celebrating that season.

## Principles

Two principles need to guide the process of selecting seasonal service music. First, the music chosen should express the specific character of the season. Begin by considering the liturgical year, both as a whole and in its individual seasons. Why does the Church follow a liturgical year? What relationship exists between the unfolding seasons and solemnities of the liturgical year and the identity and mission of the Church? Why, in the midst of the busy commercialism of pre-Christmas do we have the four weeks of Advent? Each year, why do we enter into the renewal period of Lent prior to the resurrection celebration of the weeks of Easter? What is the purpose of Ordinary Time? What formative influence does Ordinary Time bear on our growth in Christian living?

Each liturgical season has its unique identity. Advent is directed towards the coming of Christ, both at the fullness of the messianic end time and in the here-and-now of today. Advent, then, is a season of preparation and expectation, of hope-filled joy, of patient yet confident waiting. Christmas is the celebration of promised fulfillment, of feasting in the repeated birth of redemption. Yet, as it moves from the tender infancy stories through the martyrdom accounts of Stephen and the Holy Innocents to the baptismal commissioning of the adult Christ, it reminds us that our redemption is only completed through the mystery of death and resurrection. Lent is the season of baptismal renewal, and of the prayer, fasting and almsgiving which mark this recommitment to our Christian identity. Easter is the season of Alleluia, our octave of octaves *jubilus* in celebration of resurrection, when we are forbidden to fast, or even to kneel when praying. Ordinary Time is the season of prolonged fidelity, of our ongoing pilgrimage through Christian life, which is sometimes quiet and unremarkable, and other times turbulent and challenging.

Second, the relative elaborateness of the music as well as the use of certain optional musical elements should follow the principle of progressive solemnity.[1] The principle of progressive solemnity teaches us that not all liturgical celebrations are equal in importance, nor are all the elements of a given celebration of equal priority. Thus, the festal seasons of Advent-Christmas and Lent-Easter are more important than Ordinary Time. Solemnities such as SS. Peter and Paul and The Exaltation of the Holy Cross take precedence over Sundays of Ordinary Time. The eucharistic acclamations are more important musical elements than the *Glory to God* or the *Lamb of God*. Applying this principle to the selection of liturgical music means that more festive musical settings will be reserved for the festal seasons and the solemnities. It also means that certain options, such as the sprinkling rite, will be judiciously chosen for use on certain days or during certain seasons.

## Process

1. Select a small committee to collaborate with you. Perhaps one or two members of the choir, or one member from each of the choirs active in the parish, a member of the parish worship commission, and one or two "persons from the pew." Keep the committee small: you want enough members to generate a mix of input but not so many that you can never reach a decision.

2. Using sections of this book (esp. chaps. 1 and 2, the section introducing part II and chap. 1 which follows) help the committee to articulate a clear vision of what liturgical music is and what its role is meant to be in terms of liturgical prayer.

3. Discuss with them the liturgical seasons, their characteristics, and their relationship to the liturgical year as a whole and to the life and identity of the Church.

4. Make a wall chart of the liturgical year, marking the seasons and their musical elements. The chart given at the end of this chapter is a sample. To emphasize which music should be chosen first, the musical elements have been listed in order of priority rather than in chronological order.

5. Inventory your present parish repertoire concerning these elements. Evaluate each piece of music in that repertoire according to its suitability for the different liturgical seasons. As you select what best fits a given season, fill in the chart accordingly.

6. Note the blank spots in your chart and research new repertoire to fill these holes.

## Some Suggestions

The following suggestions are not definitive but are meant simply to demonstrate how service music can be chosen to support the rhythm of the liturgical year.

For Ordinary Time, I suggest selecting two settings and switching from one to the other at the point when the Gospel readings either portray Jesus deliberately turning his footsteps toward Jerusalem and the cross (Twenty-second Sunday, Year

A; Twenty-fourth Sunday, Year B) or indicate a shift of attention toward the end times (Twenty-fifth Sunday in Year C). Some examples of good Ordinary Time settings include Jan Vermulst's *People's Mass*, Owen Alstott's *Heritage Mass*, the *Danish Mass*, and the *St. Louis Jesuits Mass*.

For Lent you might select one of the simple Latin chant settings of the eucharistic acclamations (found in many current hymnals) or use the acclamations from David Hurd's English *New Plainsong Mass* or sing the *People's Mass* (if you are not using it for Ordinary Time).

For the festive seasons of Christmas and Easter, choose your most musically elaborate settings, ones with high rhythmic energy, full choir parts, and added instrumentation. You could use the same setting for both Advent and Christmas, but hold off on the choir parts and the added instrumentation until Christmas.

Making these selections judiciously will sometimes mean omitting parts of a Mass setting. For example, Hurd's *New Plainsong Mass* includes a *Glory to God* which would not be used during Lent. Although there is an aesthetic value to using the entirety of a Mass setting, the demands of a given liturgical season may require choosing only some elements from a setting, or combining parts of one setting with parts from another. What should never be submitted to this "cut-and-paste" approach, however, are the eucharistic acclamations—in order to preserve the integrity of the Eucharistic Prayer, it is essential that these be related in style and key.

Part of implementing the principle of progressive solemnity means making decisions about optional elements. When will you use the sprinkling rite? Certainly during the Easter season but also perhaps during Advent-Christmas. Using the sprinkling rite during both of these festal seasons would highlight their relationship to one another.

When will you sing the penitential rite? An obvious time is during the penitential season of Lent; however, the most appropriate form of the penitential rite during this season is Form A (*I confess*), which is recited. An alternative season for singing the act of penance would be Advent because of its eschatological character (but then do not use the sprinkling rite).

When might you do a prolonged Gospel procession? All of the Sundays of the Easter season would be appropriate, as would the Sundays and solemnities of the Christmas season. On Easter, Pentecost, and the Solemnity of the Most Holy Body and Blood of Christ, accompany this procession with the singing of the sequence and extend the procession throughout the body of the church. Such a combination would be most fitting since the sequences originated in the Middle Ages as extensions of the *Alleluia* verse.

When might you sing the General Intercessions? Since they are a litany it is always appropriate to do so, but you may not have the music or cantor resources to do so every Sunday. A better approach, then, is to apply the principle of progressive solemnity and sing them during the Christmas and Easter seasons, and on such solemnities as All Saints and Christ the King.

## Pacing the Process

The process of determining a yearlong cycle of seasonal settings may take some years to achieve. Once existing repertoire is earmarked for specific seasons, the task of researching and selecting settings for those seasons for which the parish has no appropriate music—and then of teaching that new repertoire—will take time. Be realistic with yourself, your committee, and your parish. Set goals: one small, achievable step at a time.

In terms of your committee, you want to avoid overwhelming them with the immensity of the project. You might subdivide the task, letting one group select eucharistic acclamations, and another decide about settings of the *Glory to God* and the *Lamb of God.* Or you might divide the work seasonally, assigning each season to a different subcommittee. It will also be helpful if you, as music director, make some prior judgments about available musical settings. Remove from consideration settings which are not appropriate musically, liturgically, or pastorally. This will facilitate the work of your committee(s) and help them more easily to accomplish their goals.

Regarding the parish, the introduction of new service music needs to be sensitively paced. Learning one new setting a year is a major achievement for most assemblies. This means that some less appropriate music will have to stay in place for a time while the whole process of establishing a year-round repertoire of seasonal service music unfolds. What is important is that you know where you are going and what steps you are taking—slowly but surely—to get there.

Regarding yourself, be patient with the size of the task and with the educational efforts it requires of you. Keep the goal in front of you, and think of the long term. In the meantime, enjoy the process as it unfolds. You will be teaching the parish a great deal about the liturgical year and the importance of its rhythms; you will be collaborating with a number of parish members in establishing a solid parish repertoire of service music; you will be fulfilling the most important aspect of your ministry as a liturgical musician: leading the assembly to deeper participation in the paschal mystery through the mystery and ministry of music.

## Note

[1] General Instruction of the Liturgy of the Hours, §273.

| | ADVENT | CHRISTMAS | LENT | EASTER | ORDINARY TIME I | ORDINARY TIME II |
|---|---|---|---|---|---|---|
| **Eucharistic Acclamations:** Holy, Holy | | | | | | |
| Memorial Acclamation | | | | | | |
| Great Amen | | | | | | |
| **Gospel Acclamations:** Extended Procession | | | | | | |
| Sequence | ■ | ■ | ■ | Easter Pentecost | [Body and Blood of Christ] | [Sorrowful Mother] |
| Glory to God | ■ | | ■ | | | |
| Lamb of God | | | | | | |
| Penitential Rite | | | | ■ | | |
| Sprinkling Rite | | | ■ | | | |
| Sung General Intercessions | | | | | | |

# Selecting a Parish
# Music Resource

The following pages outline a process for selecting a liturgical music resource for your parish or community. The process needs to be based on an understanding of liturgy as the ritual enactment of the paschal mystery, that is, the mystery of Jesus Christ's entire life, death, resurrection, ascension, sending of the Spirit, and future eschatological coming—*and* our participation in that mystery through the demands of daily Christian living. In celebrating liturgy we—the Body of Christ—surrender to that mystery. We are also given the nourishment and strength we need to do so.

As with all the actions, gestures, words, and movements of liturgy, music is meant to further this surrender to an enactment of the paschal mystery. Far from being entertainment, music plays a demanding role in liturgy. It must provide nourishment which is lasting and formative rather than superficial and passing. The musical resource we choose to place in our pews says something about our liturgical understanding and commitment. It is not neutral.

## Hierarchy of Evaluation

Use the hierarchy of musical forms given in chapter 2 of this book to guide your process. Since the acclamations are the most important sung element in the eucharistic rite, look first at the service music. What does the resource offer? Are the settings well-crafted musically? Are they singable for *this* assembly? Is there a variety of styles which will help you establish a cycle of settings appropriate to the different seasons of the liturgical year? If not, can you supplement these offerings easily, for example, with another resource, or with settings already well known by the assembly? Perhaps all you need from a given resource is access to a setting not already in your parish repertoire. Remember, the goal is eventually to have seasonal sets of service music in place which support the unfolding of the liturgical year (see chap. 8). No single music resource needs to contain them all—one of your supplemental resources is the collective memory of the assembly.

Next examine the psalm settings. The psalms have many uses—in the Liturgy of the Word, in Morning and Evening Prayer, and in private devotional prayer. What does this resource offer? In addition to paraphrased translations—which are suitable for liturgical moments such as the Communion procession—does the resource include the Lectionary texts intended for use in the Liturgy of the Word? Are the musical settings well-crafted? Are they able to be sung by *this* assembly? Are they settings which will stand the test of time? Are they able to be sung year after year? Or are they facile melodies which will soon become tiresome?

Look next at the hymns. Is the language contemporary rather than archaic? Is the language inclusive rather than exclusive? Is the collection culturally inclusive? Do the texts support liturgical rather than private prayer? (This does not mean that a resource should not include hymns for private devotional use but that these should not predominate.) What balance of the familiar and the new is offered? Of the new, are they texts and tunes which will stand the test of time or are they "passing fancies"?

Check what music is included besides music for the eucharistic rite. Is there music for other sacramental celebrations? For RCIA rites? For Morning and Evening Prayer? In other words, how helpful is this resource for the total liturgical life of the parish?

Check what indexes are included. In addition to the alphabetical listing of first lines and common titles, a "knowledgeable" hymnal today includes a metrical index; a tune index; a liturgical index; a topical index; an index of hymns according to the liturgical year; an index of psalm refrains; an index of Scripture passages related to hymns; an index of composers, authors, and sources; and a listing of acknowledgments. All of these enable a more intelligent use of the contents of the resource.

Finally, evaluate the format and appearance of the resource. How are its contents organized? Is the service music in an easily identifiable and prominent place? Are the hymns ordered according to the liturgical year? Is the layout easy to look at and follow? Is the paper of good quality? Is the cover attractive and durable?

## Pacing the Process

The steps outlined above are simple but they cannot be done quickly. The choice of a music resource will be a better one if it has been given sufficient time and if a number of persons in the parish or community have participated in making it. It is not realistic to have everyone in the parish or community involved, but it is very important to use a representative group: the music director, a member of the liturgy committee, one or two members of each of the choirs, one or two representatives from each age group—from teenagers to senior citizens—and representatives from the various cultural/racial groups who make up the parish. Part of the task will be to lead this group to a knowledge of liturgy and liturgical music so that their discussions will proceed from informed opinion rather than just personal likes and dislikes.

The task needs to be divided into manageable segments. Never meet for more than sixty to seventy-five minutes—beyond that time limit, people rush to decisions because they are tired and want to get home! Use the steps outlined above to organize the discussion; use segments from relevant chapters in this book to assist the group.

For your first session, talk about liturgy as enactment of the paschal mystery. This is the foundational session and the content needs to be carefully and fully addressed. Use chaps. 1 and

2 of this book as your resource. End the session by giving the group some personal reflection to do. For example, tell them to come to the next meeting prepared to share how what they learned at this meeting affected the way they participated in Sunday Eucharist.

For the second session deal just with the acclamations (see chap. 3). What are they? Why are they the most important musical element in the liturgy? What is the assembly doing when they sing them? Why have seasonal sets? Once the group has developed an understanding of acclamations and their role, evaluate the service music in the music resources you are considering. Make a chart in which you keep a running evaluation of the resources for comparison as you progress.

In your third meeting evaluate the psalm settings (see chap. 5). What is the role of the responsorial Psalm in the Liturgy of the Word? What criteria make for a "good" responsorial Psalm setting? What do the music resources you are considering have to offer? What is your evaluation of these offerings?

The fourth discussion can focus on the hymns (see chap. 4). When are hymns used in the liturgy? What are their different functions? What makes a hymn "good"? How does one evaluate a hymn musically and textually?

The remaining three segments—music for rites other than the Eucharist, the indexes, the resource's format and appearance—can probably be considered at one meeting. What is the usefulness of this resource beyond music for the Mass? What does the physical construction and appearance of the book say about the value and place of liturgy in the life of the Church?

By this time your committee will have a very full chart to see! The question now will be to compare the relative values of the resources you have been examining. Which one(s) will enable this parish to enter more deeply into the celebration of liturgy as ritual enactment of the paschal mystery? Which one(s) will both help you build on past tradition and take you into the future? Which one(s) will deepen your sense of identity as the Body of Christ as well as expand it?

## Concluding Remark

No one musical resource will contain everything a given assembly needs. Compromises will have to be made, and no matter what you select supplemental resources will be needed. But the very choosing of a resource, and the process by which you choose it, is itself a symbol of the importance of liturgy, of its dynamism at the center of the Church's life, of the care with which we approach the celebration of liturgy, and of the care with which we nurture the assembly's participation in the liturgy. This is, after all, what we are singing about.

# A Paschal Mystery
# Spirituality for
# Liturgical Musicians

The core of Christian liturgy, and its structural underpinning, is the paschal mystery, the mystery of Christ continuing to die and rise in us his Body for the sake of the life of the world (see Rom 6:3-11).

In liturgy we enact the death and resurrection of Christ as present, ongoing event. This death and resurrection is not external to us who celebrate it but is instead the very substance of our Christian identity and living. Through liturgy we identify the paschal mystery as our mystery, and choose to surrender to its call. This understanding is the deepest meaning of the Constitution on the Sacred Liturgy's mandate concerning full, conscious, and active participation of all the faithful in the liturgy.[1]

## What We Are Singing

If liturgy is ritual enactment of our identity and mission as Body of Christ called to paschal mystery living, then what we are singing when we celebrate liturgy is the paschal mystery itself and the pattern which this mystery lays out for our lives. Our very singing is a ritual embodiment of this mystery and entering into the singing is an act of entering into the mystery.

It is no accident that we participate in this ritual of transformation by singing it. Dynamics inherent to singing enable paschal mystery enactment because they open us up to the mystery and pattern us after its dying and rising. The first thing our singing does is make us present to the liturgical action. All sound communicates presence.[2] Even sound we classify as simply noise registers in our awareness as presence. Hence we cease work at our desk to investigate the nibbling we hear in the kitchen cupboard. Even things invisible and unseen (a creek at the far side of the forest; a baby crying next door) become present to us when we hear them. Sound which is word reveals personal presence (is not the proclaimed Word the presence of Christ?), and sound which is song manifests even fuller presence. This is so because of a dual and seemingly contradictory phenomenon we experience when we sing. Sound is embodied, issuing from within a physical source, but it is also disembodied because it leaves its source behind. The result is that singing generates within us a feeling of "at-placeness"—of body awareness which is self-awareness and a simultaneous feeling of being beyond our body. When we sing we become aware of being here-and-now while at the same time being over-there-and-beyond. We expand into surrounding space and fill it. We become immensely present. In terms of liturgy, singing enables us to enter the ritual enactment, to be here and not somewhere else and to be here in a significant way.

Second, our singing makes us present to one another. Sound reveals interiority. (Do we not thump on a melon to discern if it is ripe?) When the sound heard is voice, the interiority is that of a person. Thus, to speak is a radical choice to make oneself present. Speaking is revelation of the unseen dimensions of one's self, and singing reveals even more of what is hidden because it originates at a deeper physical point in the body's vocalization mechanism. The tones which make up song flow from a deeper place within the vocal tract (the throat) than do the consonants of speech. This means that on a purely physiological plane more of our self is released in song than in speech, more of our interiority revealed. In terms of liturgy, singing opens the floodgate whereby we hold nothing personal back from Christ and the community as we engage in this enactment of our baptismal identity.

Third, our singing unleashes our power as Body of Christ. Part of what is perceived in the here-and-now actuality of sound is the use of power: the babbling of the creek discloses the force of water in motion; the crying of the baby reveals the exertion of diaphragm and lungs. Sound reveals presence, and it is always a presence bearing power. When the sound which is heard is word, the power exhibited goes far beyond the physical level involved in its production: the wailing of the baby manifests the efforts of this fledgling self to wield influence over its environment. Word reveals power in the act of determining both self and world.

This is why oral societies conceive of language as a mode of action. Words have power because sound by its nature signals the use of power. Thus Scripture understands word (in Hebrew, *dabar*) as event, as effective, real, and powerful. The divine word commanded, "Let it be!" and the world sprung into existence. Christ commanded, "Lazarus, come out!" (John 11:43; Fifth Sunday of Lent, Year A) and the dead man sprung back to life.

Word is manifestation of power because it is event; it is also manifestation of power because it expresses otherwise hidden will and intention. The first level of this will and intention is the very choice to speak. As the musical theorist David Burrows puts it:

> We cannot choose to have no visual appearance. . . . But we can choose to have no auditory appearance at all simply by remaining silent, and this imparts a special quality to the moment we do commit ourselves to speech, or song, or any other sound. The voice . . . is always . . . a manifestation of will and intention.[3]

In a given acoustic space where sound binds multiple presences and interiorities to one another through shared vibration and resonance, voice becomes the calling of one consciousness to another in the dynamics of confrontation and communication, speech a participation in the mutuality of power. Voice plays a defining role in liturgical enactment of the paschal mystery because through it we actualize Christian identity by articulating communal will and intention. Through voice we choose to place our personal power at the service of the communal endeavor, the liturgical reentry into our Christian identity. In terms of liturgy this choice comes through a negotiation of forces and resistances brought into balance most patently in the ritual action of communal song, for speech united to music both projects power and harmonizes its competing forces.

Fourth, our singing transforms resistance into grace. When we understand liturgy as ritual enactment of our participation in the paschal mystery, we realize that this participation is going to make great demands of us—not only within the liturgical celebration but in our daily lives. It is not surprising that we resist this challenge. The miracle of music, as with all sound, is that it requires resistance in order to exist—for all sound is the product of force meeting resistance.[4] Wind pushes through a crack in the eves; footsteps clomp down a hallway; a finger thumps a melon. In all cases both the force and something resisting the force are necessary for sound to occur.

The specific sound which is voice results from the resistance of the larynx to pressure exerted by breath pushed out of the lungs by the diaphragm. When sound becomes voice the dialectic of force-resistance is projected onto the playing field of human relationships. Voice becomes the force of the self meeting the resistance of the other (and vice versa: voice becomes the resistance of the self to the force of the other).[5] We use voice to stake claim, to ward off, to defend, to fence out. In liturgy we actualize our choice to be Church through this very rubbing together of personal forces and resistances. We deal with our resistance to being Body of Christ—one community without claims, without private territory, without exclusions—by using the very resistance inherent in the voicing of song. In the physiological act of singing, when breath flows freely through an open throat, the force and resistance involved in producing sound operate in perfect balance, and we feel release. We feel ourselves open up. Resistance is not eliminated—it is necessary for song to happen—but it is transformed from barricade to bridge.

*What* we sing in liturgy, then, is our identity as Body of Christ called to paschal mystery living. By the power of the dynamics written into its nature, liturgical singing enacts this identity within and among us. In our liturgical singing we become Body of Christ open to God's ritual transformation of us, open to one another and empowered by the transformation of our resistances to live the dying and rising paschal mystery in the mission of daily life.

## A Paschal Mystery Spirituality of Liturgical Music

The power of song in liturgy to fulfill its ritual nature, however, is neither automatic nor guaranteed. The conundrum of music is that it can also be the first thing to sidetrack us from the core of the liturgy. Sometimes the failure is the music itself, poorly written or poorly "texted." Sometimes the failure is our use of the music, well written, well "texted," but misplaced in the rite. And sometimes the failure is in our own timorous hearts. The power of song to "do its liturgical job," so to speak, is directly related to our willingness to live the paschal mystery.

When the music pulls us *away from* the ritual action drawing us instead either to itself or to ourselves this is telling us that we as assembly or as musical leaders (organist, instrumentalist, choir member, cantor, etc.) are not allowing God's grace to transform our natural resistances to the paschal mystery. The core of this mystery is dying to self, and none of us deliberately seeks this out. And so instead of choosing self as Body of Christ we choose self as musical performer. There is a tension here, for the ability to lead music in worship (i.e., to stand before an assembly and to sing a psalm; to play an instrument in public, etc.) takes performance ego. How do we allow this ego to be subsumed into the ego of Christ? There is a dying to self here. Or instead of choosing self as Body of Christ we choose to stay locked in the world of our private relationship with God. There is a tension here, for this private world is essential to authentic Christian living, but it is not the world we are called to enter when we gather for liturgy. The call is to surrender to our relatedness to one another, to our common identity as Church. There is a dying to self here.

When the music pulls us *away from* the ritual action this is telling us that we may be choosing only music which will entertain us, make us feel good. There is a tension here, for "feeling good" can be a result of prayer. This is the most frequent argument I encounter in favor of using contemporary Christian music in liturgy: this music moves us to prayer. The purpose of music in liturgy, however, is not to make us *feel* religious, but to make us *be* religious[6] and this does not always feel good at all. We are talking here about passions deeper than the passing moment, about the passion that keeps a spouse day after day, week after week at the bedside of a terminally ill husband or wife; about the passion that keeps a Nelson Mandela in prison for twenty-seven years; about the passion that leads a Dietrich Bonhoeffer to his death; about the passion in ordinary, everyday life that leads a mother to change a dirty diaper and a father to apologize to a son he has hurt. There is a dying to self here.

When the music pulls us *away from* the ritual action it may be, beautiful as it is, the wrong music. There is a tension here, for the same music which enables one community to enter the ritual may impede another. Joseph Gelineau has often argued that the most beautifully constructed Bach chorale can be the worst liturgical choice for an assembly for whom, for whatever reasons, such music does not speak liturgically. Or the music may be liturgically potent but performed so poorly that it impedes rather than supports liturgical participation. There are two issues here: What music is in fact liturgical music? (That is, to what is the Church and the liturgy calling us?) And also, What music helps this community here enter the rite? (That is, to what is this community calling us?) Answering these questions challenges us to know the rite, know the nature of liturgy, and know the character and culture of our local community. There will be a dying to self here.

On the other hand the music will pull us *into* the ritual enactment when we have helped our parish develop a "durable and ample body of ritual music."[7] There is a tension here, for the task calls us to grow in our liturgical understanding and to surrender our preferences to the broader vision of the Church. There will be some music you and I love which will need to be "retired" from the repertoire, and there will be the endless and challenging task of forming the assembly in liturgical prayer and spirituality. It is far easier to teach new and entertaining music than it is to form people in liturgical prayer. There will be dying to self here.

The music will pull us *into* the ritual action when we allow the assembly to be the primary liturgical musicians. There is a tension here, for we who are professional musicians and presiders must move over. But this makes our position more important, not less so. Ours is the task of identifying where the real song of Christ arises, what that song is about, and how we can encourage and strengthen that song. There is a dying to self here.

## A Paschal Mystery Spirituality for Liturgical Musicians

What shapes all liturgical spirituality—and this includes the spirituality of liturgical music—is the call to paschal mystery living which arises out of our baptismal identity as Body of Christ. This mystery—our participation through baptism in the death and resurrection of Christ (see Rom 6:3-11)—is at the core of Christian life and liturgy and is at the heart of our ministry as liturgical musicians. But what is this mystery of dying and rising in Christ? How do we define it? Where do we encounter it? Most importantly, how do we as liturgical musicians surrender to it and make it the fundamental agenda that shapes our liturgical music choices?

**Defining the mystery.** The paschal mystery is simply the choice to surrender our will to the will of God. Such choice always requires a dying to self. And it always results in deeper, freer, more redeemed life. We very easily see this as the mystery of Christ's life but not so easily as the mystery of our own life. But this is exactly what Paul invites us to see: that the mystery of baptism is precisely the intertwining of Christ's dying and rising with our own. The paschal mystery defines our life as much as it defined Christ's. This means that the paschal mystery is not a past event but a present one. We participate with Christ in this mystery and in doing so we collaborate with him in bringing about redemption for the whole world.

We can understand more about this mystery by examining how it was present in Jesus' life. For one thing, the mystery of dying and rising encompassed the entirety of his life, not just the moments of Good Friday and Easter Sunday. In fact the mystery began with Mary and her *yes* to a very difficult, painful, and challenging request on the part of God. The mystery continued in Jesus' own willingness to be formed by Mary (and Joseph) in faith, values, and behavior. It was present in his continual encounters with the sick, the suffering, the poor, and the hungry; in his struggles and frustrations with his disciples; and in his ongoing confrontations with some religious authorities. In every situation, at every moment, Jesus chose to die to himself so that God's desires for humankind could be fulfilled.

A second characteristic of the paschal mystery which we see from reflecting on Jesus'—and Mary's—experience is that dying to self and rising to new life occur not only at dramatic moments such as the Annunciation and the Crucifixion but also during the ordinary moments of daily life. Mary's *yes* to God's request that she become the mother of the Savior brought long years of raising a child who, like all children, needed careful and conscientious parenting. My own mother, who raised eleven children, has a favorite picture of Mary (Max Ernst's *Die Jungfrau züchtigt das Jesuskind vor drei Zeugen*, 1926) in which Mary's traditional blue garb has slipped off her shoulders to her knees to reveal a bright red undergarment. What we see is no soft young girl but a passionate woman. And one who has a job to do—she has Jesus upended on her lap and is administering quite a spanking! His cheeks are pink, but these are not the ones we are used to seeing in a Madonna and Child painting. While her halo glows above her head, his has fallen off and rolled over to the wall.

What we see portrayed in this painting is not only the humanness of Jesus but more importantly the ordinariness and the "ongoingness" of the demands of the paschal mystery. Every day Mary had to make choices which kept her faithful to the role God was calling her to play in redemption. These choices came through the ordinary circumstances of living, loving, and relating. In making these choices she taught Jesus the pattern of the paschal mystery.

**Living the mystery.** We too encounter the paschal mystery most immediately in the ordinary living of daily life, in the ordinary demands of what it means to live consciously as a faithful Christian. Often we are not aware of the paschal mystery potential of ordinary daily life because we mistakenly equate the paschal mystery only with dramatic death-resurrection events. But as we have been pointing out, the mystery of dying to self and rising to new life in Christ is ongoing and ordinary. It comes to us in the faces of those whom we know well, in the situations we deal with at work, and in the neighborhood needs which knock on our door.

As liturgical musicians we encounter the paschal mystery and surrender to its transforming grace in numerous concrete, ordinary, and ongoing ways. For example, every time we choose to use music to lead the assembly to Christ rather than to ourselves we are surrendering to the paschal mystery. Every time we conscientiously select music best suited to help this assembly pray the liturgy rather than music which will only entertain we are surrendering to the paschal mystery. We die to ourselves every time we arrive on time and prepared for liturgy, every time we stay late because more rehearsal is required, every time we remain faithful to the disciplined preparation liturgical music requires. We surrender whenever we remain present to the liturgical action even when this is our fourth Mass of the day. We die to ourselves both whenever we persevere in the hard task of helping the choir sound better and whenever we accept with patience the best sound they can give.

When we die to ourselves in these ways the rising of Christ is heard in the stronger, more prayerful singing of the assembly. The rising of Christ is felt in the assembly's deeper participation in the liturgy. The rising of Christ is experienced in the greater compassion choir members show one another and the increased sense of dignity they feel about themselves.

Paradoxically, one of the most telling indications that we as liturgical musicians are choosing to die and rise with Christ will be the presence of silence within the assembly. This is paradoxical because we tend to measure our success in terms of noise level. I am not referring here to full-bodied assembly singing—that is a good sign. But even the most energetic, upbeat singing of an assembly that has been led to surrender to Christ will convey a dimension of silence that can be heard beneath the notes. This silence is the manifestation of their presence to prayer, to Christ, to one another as Body of Christ. This silence is the inaudible sound of their surrender to the mystery which shapes their lives. An assembly which has entered this level of silence will not wish to break it with applause.

And here we as musicians enter another level of dying to self, for an assembly focused on Christ will not be paying attention to us. I often tell cantors, for example, that one sign they are leading the assembly to pray the responsorial Psalm is that they will find themselves being complimented less frequently for the beauty of their voice. They will simply have become transparent. But is not such transparency the goal of all liturgical prayer and of the music which supports it? We must decrease so that Christ may increase. There is a dying to self here. But, oh, what a rising, not only for this assembly but for the whole world!

## Notes

[1] CSL §14.

[2] In this section I draw on the work of two scholars, Walter J. Ong, S.J. (*The Presence of the Word: A Prolegomena for Cultural and Religious History* [Yale University Press, 1967]; *Orality and Literacy: The Technologizing of the Word* [Methuen, 1982; reprint, Routledge, 1988]) and David Burrows (*Sound, Speech and Music* [University of Massachusetts Press, 1990]), who explore the relationship of sound and voice to communication of presence, interiority, and power.

[3] Burrows, 31.

[4] See Burrows, 23.

[5] See Burrows, 31–32; 12.

[6] See Mark Searle, "Ritual and Music: A Theory of Liturgy and Implications for Music," *Assembly* 12, no. 3 (1986).

[7] Don Saliers, "Liturgical Music Formation" in *Liturgy and Music: Lifetime Learning*, ed. Robin A. Leaver and Joyce Ann Zimmerman, C.PP.S. (Collegeville, Minn.: The Liturgical Press, 1998) 392.